Law of
ATTRACTION

Law of
ATTRACTION

The Science of Attracting More of What You Want
and Less of What You Don't

Michael J. Losier

**WELLNESS
CENTRAL**

NEW YORK   BOSTON

This Wellness Central edition is published by arrangement with
Michael J. Losier Enterprises, Inc. Victoria, British Columbia,
Canada

Wellness Central
Hachette Book Group
237 Park Avenue
New York, NY 10017

www.HachetteBookGroup.com

Printed in the United States of America

Orignally published in hardcover by Hachette Book Group.

First Wellness Central Edition: June 2007
First Trade Edition: May 2010
10 9 8 7 6 5 4 3

Wellness Central is an imprint of Grand Central Publishing.
The Wellness Central name and logo are trademarks of Hachette
Book Group, Inc.

ISBN 978-0-446-19973-5 (pbk.)
LCCN: 2007926456

Law of
ATTRACTION

able of Contents

hat Others Are Saying
bout This Book

_ichael Losier's message will change the way you view yourself and
ers. I found_ Law of Attraction _both inspiring and healing."_

>Ethelle G. Lord, M.Ed., CCG
>Teamwork Development Associates
>www.teamworkcoaching.com

_ichael Losier has a gift for being able to distill abstract principles into
ults that work._ Law of Attraction _is easy to read, easy to apply, and
t of all, it really works!"_

>Mary Marcdante, Speaker,
>Author of _My Mother, My Friend_
>www.marymarcdante.com

_you want to really understand why your life is the way it is and if you
lly want to know how you can change it to anything you want, here is
instruction book, and it is in plain language."_

>Mark Foster, Wigan UK

_e read other Law of Attraction books but something seemed to be
ssing. Losier provides the missing piece through his Clarity Through
ntrast and Desire Statement worksheets."_

>Janet Boyer, New Age Editor
>www.NewAgeBellaOnline.com

_hat an outstanding book! Michael's short and simple formula for
racting anything your heart desires will work big time for he or she
t follows it. I highly recommend you apply his principles in your life
achieve mega success!"_

>Zev Saftlas, Author of _Motivation That Works_
>and founder of www.EmpoweringMessages.com

"This book supports the proposition that simplicity is the best design. Short and simple, the author provides a good working outline of the principles underlying the Law of Attraction and then provides practical exercises to assist the reader in utilizing them."

Antigone W., Amazon.com Reader

"You may have heard about the Law of Attraction and read about it before. Michael takes the understanding of the Law of Attraction and presents it crisply and simply, in a way that anyone can hear it and understand it, from someone brand new to the Law of Attraction to the most experienced. An easy, delightful read!"

Eva Gregory, Amazon.com Reader
Author of *The Feel Good Guide to Prosperity*

"Totally by chance, I was extremely fortunate to see Michael Losier present his "Law of Attraction" seminar. Michael is an entertaining, dynamic, and honest speaker, and his teachings have changed my life. As an upbeat and positive person, I was extremely surprised to learn how much of my daily self-talk was actually sabotaging my efforts to attract the type of relationships and things I wanted in life (and I've read hundreds of other personal development books by today's top gurus). Michael's methods are far more than positive affirmations or fluffy new age mantras. His material is practical, easily learned, and although deceptively simple, it is extremely powerful. The Law of Attraction *book is a great value, and I highly recommend it to anyone who is interested in increasing his or her quality of life."*

John Goudie, Youth at Risk Counsellor

"Out of all the books, tapes, and resources that I've purchased on the topic of "creating your ideal life," Michael Losier's Law of Attraction *is the absolute best "nuts-and-bolts" treatment I've ever read. Period. What Losier teaches in this book is NOT how to become someone who attracts results – you're already doing that. Instead, he teaches you, in plain English with no weird jargon, how to become a DELIBERATE attractor and start consciously attracting more of the things you want out of life and less of the things you don't want. This book has my highest recommendation. If I couldn't get another copy, I wouldn't take $1,000 for mine."*

Tony Rush, Life Coach, Alabama

A Brief History of the Law of Attraction

Some of you have heard reference to the Law of Attraction from various sources while others are just beginning to learn about it. In modern times the Law of Attraction has been documented since the early 1900s. Here's a brief history:

1906 - Atkinson, William Walter
Thought Vibration or the Law of Attraction in the Thought World

1926 - Holmes, Ernest
Basic Ideas of Science of Mind

1949 - Holliwell, Dr. Raymond
Working with the Law

In the early 1990s, information and teachings on the Law of Attraction became widely available through the publications of Jerry and Esther Hicks. (Refer to their website for all current teachings/papers – www.abraham-hicks.com.) It is through their teachings that I really "got it."

Since 2000, many articles and books have been written about the Law of Attraction, and its appeal has expanded to a much broader audience. The future holds many more authors and teachers writing on this topic as the message of the Law of Attraction continues to grow in its mass appeal.

What Makes This Book Different?

In 1995 I studied NLP (Neuro Linguistic Programming) to understand how our mind and thoughts work. This led me to many insights on how people learn. You'll notice while reading this book that it appeals to your and others' reading style. This book is written in such a way that each section builds on the l and as in any training manual, you can use the tools, exercises and scripts to keep you connected to the Law of Attraction.

Many of the books I've studied were broad in their theoretical approach to the subject of the Law of Attraction. Nowhere co I find an answer to my question, "How do I actually DO this? With my knowledge of NLP and how to teach using different learning styles, I created an easy-to-follow HOW-TO book for students of the Law of Attraction. Using the exercises and too in this book, you will be able to learn quickly so you can begin practicing the Law of Attraction in your own life.

The most frequent and satisfying compliment I receive is that book is SIMPLE to read and the exercises are easy to follow. T book has been embraced by a multitude of different religious and spiritual groups. In addition, it has become required readi for many sales groups, network marketing companies, realtors, financial advisors and other business organizations. In short, th book has mass appeal.

ou're Already Experiencing ~~~~~ e Law of Attraction

Have you noticed that sometimes what you need just falls into place or comes to you from an out-of-the-blue telephone call? Or you've bumped into someone on the street you've been thinking about? Perhaps you've met the perfect client or life partner, just by fate or being at the right place at the right time. All of these experiences are evidence of the Law of Attraction in your life.

Have you heard about people who find themselves in bad relationships over and over again, and who are always complaining that they keep attracting the same kind of relationship? The Law of Attraction is at work for them too.

The Law of Attraction may be defined as: *I attract to my life whatever I give my attention, energy and focus to, whether positive or negative.* By reading this book you'll come to understand why and how this happens.

There are a number of words or expressions that describe eviden of the Law of Attraction. If you've ever used any of these words expressions you're actually referring to the Law of Attraction.

Here are just a few:

- ◆ Out-of-the-blue
- ◆ Serendipity
- ◆ Coincidence
- ◆ Fate
- ◆ Karma
- ◆ Fell into place
- ◆ Synchronicity
- ◆ Luck
- ◆ Meant to be

In this book you'll learn why these experiences happen. More importantly, you'll discover how you can use the Law of Attraction more deliberately. You'll be able to attract all that you need to do, know and have, so you can get more of what you want and less of what you don't want. As a result, you'll ha your ideal client, your ideal job, your ideal relationship, your ideal vacation, your ideal health, more money in your life, and all that you desire. Really!

e Science of the
w of Attraction

There is a physiological foundation for positive thinking and its effect in creating the Law of Attraction.

There are many forms of energy: atomic, thermal, electromotive, kinetic and potential. Energy can never be destroyed.

You may also recall that all matter is made up of atoms, and that each atom has a nucleus (containing protons and neutrons), around which orbit electrons.

Electrons in atoms always orbit the nucleus in prescribed "orbitals" or energy levels that assure the stability of the atom. Electrons may be compelled to assume "higher" orbits by the addition of energy, or may give off energy when they drop to a "lower" orbit. When it comes to "vibrations," if atoms are "aligned," they create a motive force, all pulling together in the same direction in much the same way as metals can be magnetized by aligning their molecules in the same direction. This creation of positive (+) and negative (–) poles is a fact of nature and science. Suffice to say, science has shown that if there are physical laws that can be observed and quantified in one arena, there are most probably similar laws in other arenas, even if they cannot be quantified at this time.

So you see, the Law of Attraction isn't a fancy term or new-age magic. It is a law of nature that every atom of your being is in constant response to, whether you know it or not.

For readers who want to find out more about the connection between energy, our thoughts and the world of 'matter' around us, I recommend watching the movie, What the Bleep Do We Know © 2004 Captured Light & Lord of the Wind Films, LLC.

aking Reference to
e Law of Attraction

Many authors have written about the Law of Attraction. Here are just a few of the many ways the Law of Attraction has been referred to in various books.

That which is like unto itself is drawn.
> Jerry and Esther Hicks, *(The Teachings of Abraham) Ask and It Is Given*

What you radiate outward in your thoughts, feelings, mental pictures and words, you attract into you life.
> Catherine Ponder, *Dynamic Law of Prosperity*

Never expect a thing you do not want, and never desire a thing you do not expect. When you expect something you do not want, you attract the undesirable, and when you desire a thing that is not expected, you simply dissipate valuable mental force. On the other hand, when you constantly expect that which you persistently desire, your ability to attract becomes irresistible. The mind is a magnet and attracts whatever corresponds to its ruling state.
> Dr. Raymond Holliwell, *Working with the Law 11 Truth Principles for Successful Living*

Every thought must manifest according to its intensity. The slightest thought of Intelligence sets in motion a power in the Law to produce a corresponding thing.
> Ernst Holmes, *Basic Ideas of Science of Mind*

You are a living magnet; you attract into your life people, situations and circumstances that are in harmony with your dominant thoughts. Whatever you dwell on in the conscious grows in your experience.
> Brian Tracy

Definition of the Law of Attraction

I attract to my life whatever I give my attention, energy and focus to, whether positive or negative.

The word *vibe* is often used to describe a mood or a feeling that you pick up from someone or something. For example, you may say you pick up a *good vibe* when you are around a certain person. Or you may say that you get a *negative vibe* when you walk in a certain part of a city or neighbourhood. In all of these cases, the word *vibe* is used to describe the mood or feeling you are experiencing. In short, a *vibe* equals a mood or a feeling.

The word *vibe* comes from the longer word vibration (which isn't used often by most people). In the 'vibrational' world, there are only two kinds of vibrations, positive (+) and negative (–). Every mood or feeling causes you to emit, send-out or offer a vibration, whether positive or negative. If you go through the dictionary and select every word that describes a feeling, you would be able to put them into either of these two categories. Each word will describe a feeling that generates a positive vibration or describe a feeling that generates a negative vibration.

Each one of us sends out either a positive or negative vibration. In fact, we are always sending a vibration. Think about the expression "He gives off good vibes," or "This neighbourhood gives me negative vibes."

On the following page you'll see examples of feelings that generate positive or negative vibrations.

Vibrations (feelings)

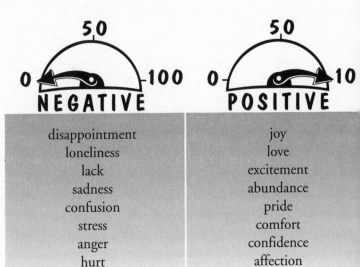

NEGATIVE	POSITIVE
disappointment	joy
loneliness	love
lack	excitement
sadness	abundance
confusion	pride
stress	comfort
anger	confidence
hurt	affection

Every single moment you have a mood or a feeling. In this moment right now, the mood or feeling you are experiencing i causing you to emit or send out a negative or positive vibratio

Here's where the Law of Attraction comes in. The Law of Attraction (universal energy around you that obeys the science of physics) is responding to the vibration you are offering. Rig now, in this very moment, it is matching your vibration by giving you more of the same, whether positive or negative.

For example, when a person wakes up first thing Monday morning feeling a little bit cranky and irritated, they are sending out a negative vibration. And while they are sending out this negative vibration, the Law of Attraction responds, matching the vibration they are sending and giving this person more of the same. (The Law of Attraction always matches your vibration – whether positive or negative.)

So, this person gets out of bed, stubs their toe, burns their toast, the traffic is snarled, a client cancels and then they catch themselves saying "I should have stayed in bed!"

Or, how about the salesperson who is joyfully excited about a huge sale they just made, thus sending out a positive vibration. Shortly after, they get another ideal sale. They catch themselves saying "I'm on a roll!"

In both of these examples the Law of Attraction is at work, unfolding and orchestrating all that needs to happen to bring them more of the same, whether positive or negative.

In this book you will learn how to identify the vibration you are sending and be able to make a conscious choice whether you want to keep sending it or change it. In the Deliberate Attraction section of this book you will learn what to do to deliberately send a different vibration. You will learn how to become a deliberate 'sender' of your vibration so that you can change the results you've been getting and have more of what you do want and less of what you don't.

The Law of Attraction responds to whatever vibration you are sending by giving you more of it, whether it's positive or negative.
It simply responds to your vibration.

on-deliberate Attraction

Many people are often curious about why they keep attracting the same thing over and over again. They are absolutely certain that they are not sending out anything negative, yet in a specific area of their life, negative experiences keep showing up. This happens because they are sending a negative vibe non-deliberately simply through their observation of what they are currently getting.

For example, if you open your wallet and don't see any money, by observing that you're not seeing any money there, you are now offering a vibration of lack, fear or some other similar negative vibration. Although you're not doing it on purpose, the Law of Attraction is simply responding to your vibration and giving you more of the same. It doesn't know what action you are taking that is causing you to generate this negative vibration. You might be remembering, or pretending, or daydreaming, or in this case just merely observing.

Observation Cycle
(Non-deliberate Attraction)

1 You observe what you receive and have in your life (whether positve or negative).

2 While observing, you are sending a vibration, either negative or positive.

3 The Law of Attraction responds to the vibration you are sending.

4 As a result, you get more of what you were vibrating, whether positive or negative.

As you observe what you are receiving in different areas of your life (money, work, health, relationships, etc.), your observation generate a feeling (vibration) that can be either positive or negative.

serving Sends a Vibration

Even though you may not be aware of it, you are perpetuating the Observation Cycle. The Law of Attraction will respond to your vibration, whether positive or negative, by giving you more of what you are vibrating.

It's important to understand that the Law of Attraction is already existing in your life whether you understand it or not, whether you like it or not, or whether you believe it or not. If you like what you are observing, then celebrate it, and in your celebration you will get more of it. If you don't like what you are getting, then it is time to tap into the Law of Attraction more deliberately so you can stop attracting what you don't want and start attracting what you do. In other words – Deliberate Attraction.

Whether it's a positive or negative vibration, the Law of Attraction will give you more of the same.

nderstanding the
gnificance of Your Words

ords, Words, Words

Most of the tools and worksheets in this book are related to language, the use of words, and more importantly, the feelings generated by words.

As you read on in this book you'll learn how words are the common denominator for all of the exercises in the Deliberate Attraction process.

hy Is There Such an Emphasis on Words?

Words are everywhere. We speak them, read them, write them, think them, see them, type them, and hear them in our head. The reason the exercises in this book are all based on choosing precise words is because the words we think and use generate the vibration we send out. The word 'homework', for example, can cause some people to have a negative vibration and others to have a positive vibration. The word 'money' can hold a positive vibration for some people and a negative vibration for others. In the following pages you'll learn which words are causing you to attract the things you don't want.

Your thoughts are made up of words. Here is an illustration showing the connection between positive and negative vibrations, your thoughts, and your words.

WORDS ➡ THOUGHTS ➡ FEELINGS
(made up of words) (negative or positive vibrations)

Words That Are Causing You to Attract What You DON'T Want

Don't, Not and No

Don't think of the Statue of Liberty in New York. I know that you just did! Your unconscious and conscious mind automatic filters out the words **don't**, **not** and **no**. When you use these words you are actually internalizing in your mind the exact thing you are being told *not* to. For example, if I said "Do not think of a snowstorm," I guarantee you would start thinking c a snowstorm almost immediately. Even though the instruction was *not* to do something, your unconscious and conscious mir edited out that part of the instruction.

There are other common expressions that give more attention and energy to what you DON'T want. Have you heard yourse use any of these statements?

Don't get mad
I'm not blaming
Don't hesitate to call me
Don't be fooled
Don't worry
I don't want this to hurt
Don't litter
Don't smoke
I'm not judging

Don't panic
No rush, no worry
Don't look now
Don't run with scissors
Don't forget
I don't want my clients
to cancel
Don't be late
Don't slam the door

The Law of Attraction responds the same way your mind does: it hears what you DON'T want. When you hear yourself make a statement containing the words **don't**, **not** or **no**, you are actually giving attention and energy to what you DON'T want.

Here's an effective and easy tool that will help you reduce and eventually eliminate the use of the words **don't**, **not** and **no** from your vocabulary. Each time you hear yourself using **don't**, **not** or **no**, ask yourself "So, what do I want?" Each time you talk about what you DON'T want, in that moment you are giving it your attention and energy. When you ask yourself what you DO want, the answer will have created a new sentence with new words. When your words change, your vibration changes, and the best news of all is that you can only send out one vibration at a time.

When you make a statement containing the words don't, not or no, you are actually giving attention and energy to what you don't want.

Simply ask yourself "SO, WHAT DO I WANT?"

When we use *don't, not* and *no,* here's how the new sentences will sound after you've asked yourself "So, what do I want?"

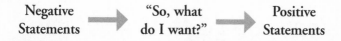

Negative Statements	"So, what do I want?"	Positive Statements

Negative Statements	Positive Statements
Don't hesitate to call	Call me soon
Don't panic	Stay calm
Don't forget	Remember to…
Don't be late	See you on time
Don't slam the door	Close it quietly
I don't want this to hurt	I'll be fine
I don't want my clients to cancel	I want my clients to keep their appointments
When do *you* use **don't, not** and **no**? Add your own sentences here. ◆ ◆ ◆ ◆ ◆	Create new positive sentences here. ◆ ◆ ◆ ◆

"Positive and negative emotions cannot occupy the mind at the same time. One or the other must dominate. It is your responsibility to make sure that positive emotions constitute the dominating influence of your mind."

Napolean Hill

When you go from what you don't want to what you do want, the words change. When the words change, the vibration changes, and you can only send out one vibration at a time.

setting Your Vibration

At every moment you can tell if the vibration you are sending is either positive or negative by identifying the feeling you are experiencing. These feelings are causing you to send out a vibration, and in the 'vibrational' world there are only two kinds of vibrations: positive and negative.

You can reset your vibration from negative to positive by simply choosing different words and different thoughts. It's as easy as asking yourself "So, what do I want?" Again, when you talk about what you don't want and then talk about what you do want, the words change. You can only send out one vibration at a time, thus

when your words change, your vibration changes too. Simply put, to reset your vibration, just change the words you're using and the thoughts you are thinking.

The Law of Attraction doesn't remember what vibration you were sending out five minutes ago, five days ago, five months ago or 50 years ago. It's only responding to the vibration you are sending out right now in this very moment and giving you more of the same.

To know whether you are sending out a positive or negative vibration, simply take a look at the results you're getting in that area of your life. They are a perfect reflection of what you are vibrating.

eliberate Attraction

In the next section you are going to discover how to use the Law of Attraction more **deliberately**. To do this, you'll learn an easy 3-step formula. In addition to learning the steps and following along with two case studies, you can participate by filling in the blank worksheets I have provided. More worksheets are available at www.LawofAttractionBook.com/worksheets.html

If you are not sure what specific area of your life you'd like to apply Deliberate Attraction to, simply choose the area that you feel the least satisfied with. It could be your relationship(s), career, health, business or your financial situation.

I recommend you finish reading the remainder of this book and then go back and do the exercises, applying them to the specific area you've chosen.

The 3-Step Formula for Deliberate Attraction

Step 1: Identify Your Desire

Sounds easy, right? Most people are not very good at knowing what they do want, however, they are very good at identifying what they don't want. In this step you'll learn why knowing what you *don't* like is helpful.

Step 2: Give Your Desire Attention

The Law of Attraction will give you more of what you give your attention, energy and focus to. This step will teach you how to do just that, simply by learning how to choose *your words*.

Step 3: Allow It

Wondering why you're not manifesting your desires? The speed at which your desires come to you depends on how much you Allowing. This is the most important step.

:ep 1 - Identify Your Desire

The first step in making the Law of Attraction work for you is to be clear about what you want. The challenge, however, is that most people are not good at knowing what they DO want but they are good at identifying what they DON'T want. Knowing what you don't want is actually good news. As you'll discover in this section, knowing what you don't want will become a helpful tool for you.

hat is Contrast?

Contrast*, as it applies to the Law of Attraction, is anything you don't like, doesn't feel good, or causes you to be in a negative mood. The moment you identify something in your life that feels like contrast and you spend time complaining about it, talking about it, or declaring that you don't want it, you are offering a negative vibration. The Law of Attraction then responds to your negative vibration by giving you more of the same.

Contrast Helpful?

Yes. By observing contrast and identifying it as something you don't want, you become clearer about what you do want. Simply ask yourself "So, what do I want?" In other words, you can use the contrast to gain clarity about what you do want by answering that question.

Take your first boyfriend or girlfriend, for example. Chances are you're no longer with that person and from that relationship you have a list of things that you didn't like. This is your list of contrast. It is this list that will help you become clear about what you do want in a partner.

* The concept of "contrast" is a distinction I learned from Jerry and Esther Hicks, Abraham-Hicks Publications.

Observing contrast is essential because it helps you to become clearer about what you do want.

hy Is It Important
Identify Contrast?

You are already experiencing clarity whenever you observe contrast in your life.

Imagine you are riding in your car with your best friend who insists on fiddling with the radio dial. Your friend chooses a heavy metal station that you hate. You begin to feel stressed.

After five seconds of the music you say to yourself "This is my car and I'm not listening to this for one second longer." You reach over and change the dial to your favorite station, which plays adult contemporary music. Instantly, you feel happier and more relaxed.

Notice how you become clear about what you like by paying attention to what you don't like? In other words, your contrast has provided you with clarity.

To help you observe contrast briefly, say, "So, what do I want?"

w Long Is Briefly?

The key to getting what you want without getting stuck focusing on what you don't want is to briefly observe contrast.

Only you can decide how long *briefly* is. For some, experiencing contrast in a relationship may last for years; for others, contrast is observed for a short time. You might decide to end a relationship on the first date.

Notice that when you experience contrast around smells, sounds, or tastes, your tolerance is minimal. Think about these statements:

How long would you smell something that doesn't smell good?
How long would you listen to music that doesn't sound good?
How long would you eat something that doesn't taste good?

In these cases, you are observing contrast briefly and changing it to clarity, FAST.

There are, however, a few areas of your life where you may observe contrast far too long:

- ◆ Relationships
- ◆ Health
- ◆ Money
- ◆ Career
- ◆ Other

Generally, the least amount of time you spend putting your attention, energy and focus toward contrast, the better. The Clarity Through Contrast process, which you'll learn from this book, will help you with this.

*Identify what makes
you feel good and
do more of it.*

ur Goal is to Limit Contrast
All Areas of Your Life

It's OK to feel good in all areas of your life. Does this sound
selfish? It's OK to be selfish when you understand that being
selfish is simply an act of self-care.

Selfish = Self-Care

- Are you selfish about what you eat?
- Are you selfish about what you smell?
- Are you selfish about what you wear?
- Are you selfish about what you listen to?

I'm encouraging you to be selfish in all areas of your life,
especially in your:

- Career
- Finances
- Health
- Relationship

In these four areas people tend to have lots of negative emotions
and observe them for a long time, in many cases, years.

The Clarity Through Contrast Process

The Clarity Through Contrast process will assist you in becoming clearer about your desires.

Here are some prominent areas in your life where clarity is beneficial:

◆ Career
◆ Money
◆ Life partner relationships
◆ Friendships
◆ Work relationships
◆ Business clients
◆ Business referrals
◆ Education
◆ Health
◆ Other

Next we'll examine two case studies that illustrate how the Clarity Through Contrast Process helped generate clarity.

se Studies

After teaching the Law of Attraction to thousands of students, I've collected wonderful stories about people whose lives have been changed working with this process. There's something about seeing someone else's story in print that really makes this tool come alive, so I've included two case studies that represent two common areas where people use the Law of Attraction to get more of what they want.

Janice's story will show you how the 3 steps, Identifying Your Desire, Giving it Attention, and Allowing can work in attracting an ideal relationship. Greg's story focuses on another difficult issue for many people – money.

Janice - Relationships

Janice, 34, is tired and frustrated because she continually has the wrong kind of guy showing interest in her. She complains that she attracts men who are unavailable, insensitive, and who seldom make her a priority.

Janice decided to use the Law of Attraction to attract her ideal relationship.

She began the process of Deliberate Attraction with Step One, Identify Your Desire, using the Clarity Through Contrast Worksheet. Take a look at Janice's worksheet on the next page.

In Janice's case, she was able to build a large list of contrast by recalling a number of past relationships, and what she didn't like (contrast) about those relationships.

Clarity Through Contrast Worksheet
Janice
My Ideal Relationship

So, what do I want?

Contrast – *things I don't like* (Side A)	Clarity – *things I like* (Side B)
1. Controlling	
2. Poor listener	
3. Not affectionate	
4. Doesn't care what I think or how I feel	
5. Not outgoing	
6. Doesn't like traveling	
7. Always rushes me	
8. Makes decisions without me	
9. Doesn't like movies or dancing	

ice made her contrast list on Side A. She recalled three past relationships ing this exercise and took a couple of days to build her list.

Clarity Through Contrast Worksheet
Janice
My Ideal Relationship

So, what do I want?

Contrast – *things I don't like* (Side A)	Clarity – *things I like* (Side B)
1. ~~Controlling~~	1. Flexible, well-balanced
2. ~~Poor listener~~	2. Great listening skills
3. ~~Not affectionate~~	3. Affectionate, sensitive
4. ~~Doesn't care what I think or how I feel~~	4. Asks me what I think and how I feel about things
5. ~~Not outgoing~~	5. He likes to meet my friends and enjoys them
6. ~~Doesn't like traveling~~	6. Enjoys social situations. Lov short-term and long-term travel, likes adventure and exploring new places togeth
7. ~~Always rushes me~~	7. Has patience, allows things unfold in due time
8. ~~Makes decisions without me~~	8. Asks for my ideas in decisio making
9. ~~Doesn't like movies or dancing~~	9. Enjoys theater, movies, love live bands and entertainmer likes dancing

Janice read each item on her list and asked herself "So, what do I want?' After she wrote the answer on Side B, she struck a line through the matching contrast on Side A.

Note: In our example we have listed 9 items on Janice's list. This exercis is most effective when you add as many items as possible to your contra: list (50-100 items). The more contrast you identify, the more clarity you generate.

Greg – Money

Greg, 27, is just barely making ends meet. He constantly complains about not having enough money. In fact, he says he's feeling stressed out about his financial situation. Greg is a self-employed consultant and business advisor, and he's having a really hard time getting and keeping clients.

He has decided to use the Law of Attraction to attract his ideal financial situation.

The Deliberate Attraction process starts with Step One, Identify Your Desire, by using the Clarity Through Contrast Worksheet. Take a look at Greg's worksheet on the next page.

Remember, in Greg's example we've listed a total of 10 items on his contrast list. This exercise is most effective when you add as many items as possible to your contrast list (50-100 items). The more contrast you identify, the more clarity you'll generate.

Clarity Through Contrast Worksheet
Greg
My Ideal Financial Situation

So, what do I want?

Contrast – *things I don't like* (Side A)	Clarity – *things I like* (Side B)
1. Not enough money	
2. Always bills to pay	
3. Just making ends meet	
4. I can't afford anything I want	
5. Money flow is sporadic	
6. I never win anything	
7. I'll always make the same amount of money	
8. Money does not come easily in my family	
9. I always struggle to pay the rent	
10. Money issues stress me	

Greg made his contrast list on Side A. He recalled his entire financial picture in the last year and took two hours to build this list. He could h taken days to complete the list if he had wanted to.

Note: In our example we have listed 10 items on Greg's list. This exercis is most effective when you add as many items as possible to your contra list (50-100 items). The more contrast you identify, the more clarity you generate.

Clarity Through Contrast Worksheet
Greg
My Ideal Financial Situation

So, what do I want?

Contrast – *things I don't like* (Side A)	Clarity – *things I like* (Side B)
~~Not enough money~~	1. An abundance of money
~~Always bills to pay~~	2. Bills are paid easily and quickly
~~Just making ends meet~~	3. Always have excess money
~~I can't afford anything I want~~	4. Always have enough money to purchase whatever I desire
~~Money flow is sporadic~~	5. Constant flow of money is coming in from multiple sources
~~I never win anything~~	6. I win prizes often; receive gifts and many free things
~~I'll always make the same amount of money~~	7. I am constantly increasing my amount of monetary intake from known and unknown sources
~~Money does not come easily in my family~~	8. Money comes easily to me
~~I always struggle to pay the rent~~	9. Rent is paid easily as I always have money
~~Money issues stress me~~	10. Money and my relationship with it feels good

g read each item on his list and asked himself "So, what do I want?"
r he wrote the answer on Side B, he struck a line through the matching
trast on Side A.

Complete Your Own
Clarity Through Contrast Worksheet

Choose an area in your life that you would like to change.

On Side A, list all of the things that are troubling you about y
situation. For example, if you are building a contrast list abou
your ideal career, your list may include "the hours are too long
or "the pay is too low." Feel free to refer to a number of past j
to help you build your list.

Take lots of time to complete this contrast list. Remember,
adding more items to your contrast list will give you more clar
I suggest you add 50-100 items. Construct it over a few days
to ensure that you have thought of all the relevant episodes of
contrast.

After you have completed building the contrast list on Side A,
read each item and ask yourself "So, what do I want?" and
complete Side B of the worksheet.

By using this Clarity Through Contrast Worksheet you will ha
a better understanding of what you do want (clarity of desire),
by listing what you don't want (contrast). After you have reach
clarity, simply cross off the matching item of contrast.

Clarity Through Contrast Worksheet
My Ideal _____

So, what do I want? ➤

Contrast – *things I don't like* (Side A)	Clarity – *things I like* (Side B)
List the things you don't like	List the things you would like

more copies of this worksheet, go to
w.LawofAttractionBook.com/worksheets.html

Clarity Through Contrast Worksheet
My Ideal _____

So, what do I want?

Contrast – *things I don't like* (Side A)	Clarity – *things I like* (Side B)

You have completed the first step of Deliberate Attraction –
Identify Your Desire.

Here's what we've covered in this section

◆ Your words generate a vibration that is either positive
   or negative.

◆ When you use the words **don't**, **not** and **no** you continue
   to give more attention, energy and focus to what you are
   referring to.

◆ When you hear yourself saying **don't**, **not** and **no** ask
   yourself "So, what do I want?"

◆ When you go from what you don't want to what you do
   want, the words change, and when the words change your
   vibration changes.

◆ You can only send out one vibration at a time.

◆ You can *reset* your vibration simply by changing your words,
   remembering that thoughts are made up of words.

◆ Contrast is anything that doesn't feel good.

◆ Observe contrast briefly knowing that the Law of Attraction
   is always responding to your vibration.

◆ Use contrast to help generate clarity.

◆ When building your contrast list find as many contrast
   items as possible. The more contrast you identify, the more
   clarity you'll have.

Remember, you've only pinpointed your desire at this point.
You may have felt great about identifying and writing down
what you want or you may have experienced a feeling of doubt.

In the following chapters, you'll learn how to continue on with
the Law of Attraction formula using Step 2 and Step 3.

tep 2 - Give Your Desire Attention

iving Attention Increases Vibration

To raise (increase) your vibration simply means to give your desire more positive attention, energy and focus.

It is not enough to merely identify your desire; you must also give it positive attention. Giving it positive attention ensures that you are including the vibration of your desire in your current vibration.

The Law of Attraction brings you more of whatever you give your attention, energy and focus to. If, however, you identify your desire and don't give it attention, energy and focus, then there is no manifestation. The key here is to identify your desire and continue to give it attention. As you're giving it attention, you are now including the vibration of your desire in your current vibration. Your current vibration is what the Law of Attraction responds to.

Some people are good at identifying their desires and then they tuck their list of desires away and never give it attention again. The Law of Attraction can only respond to what you're giving your attention to.

The next section of this book explains this concept using the idea that we have a Vibrational Bubble around us, where all of our current vibration is stored. You must be sure to include the vibration of your desire in your current Vibrational Bubble.

What am I Including in My Vibrational Bubble?

Imagine that you have a bubble that is surrounding you and captured within this bubble are all the vibrations you are sendi
out. The Law of Attraction is responding to whatever is *inside*
your Vibrational Bubble.

Are your desires inside or outside your Vibrational Bubble?

It is important to understand that all your goals, dreams and desires are outside of your Vibrational Bubble. If they were ins
your Vibrational Bubble you would already have them and be enjoying them. Take, for example, the exercise you completed
in Step 1 to identify your new desire. Now that you have new clarity about your desire, it's necessary to include that vibratior
in your current vibration because that's what the Law of Attraction responds to. If you build your desire list and put
it away in your sock drawer, your desire won't manifest because
the Law of Attraction doesn't respond to things in a sock draw
It only responds to what is currently in your Vibrational Bubbl

In Step 2 of the Deliberate Attraction process you will learn how to use words to give attention, energy and focus to your new desires by creating a Desire Statement. While you are sustaining that attention, energy and focus on your desire, you are including it in your current Vibrational Bubble where the Law of Attraction responds to and matches that vibration.

What do You include in Your Vibrational Bubbl

I Including It or Excluding It
m My Vibrational Bubble?

Using the worksheet on the following page, determine which
column each of the following sentences will go in.

- When I'm talking about what I desire
- When I'm noticing something I like
- When I'm daydreaming about my desire
- When I visualize my desire
- When I'm pretending I already have my desire
- When I say yes to something
- When I say no to something
- When I worry about something
- When I complain about something
- When I remember something positive
- When I remember something negative
- When I'm observing something positive
- When I'm observing something negative
- When I'm playing with the idea of having my desire
- When I'm making a collage about my desire
- When I'm praying about my desire
- When I'm celebrating something I like

*What am I
including in my
Vibrational Bubble?*

My Vibrational Bubble – Worksheet

Action that INCLUDES it in my Vibrational Bubble.	Action that EXCLUDES it from my Vibrational Bubble.

'll find a completed worksheet on the following page.

My Vibrational Bubble – Worksheet

Action that INCLUDES it in my Vibrational Bubble.	Action that EXCLUDES it from my Vibrational Bubble
• talking about my desire • noticing something I like • daydreaming about my desire • visualizing my desire • pretending I have my desire • when I say yes to something • when I say no to something • when I worry about something • when I complain about something • when I remember something positive • when I remember something negative • when I'm observing something positive • when I'm observing something negative • when I'm playing with the idea of having my desire • when I'm making a collage about my desire • when I'm praying about my desire • when I'm celebrating something I like	Can you see how everythin gets included?

Notice that when you say "No" to something, you just gave it attention, energy and focus. In that moment, it also becomes included in your Vibrational Bubble. Giving anything *attention of any kind* includes it in your current vibration.

Tools for Raising Your Vibration
Fuel Your Desire

One of the keys to make the Law of Attraction work for you lies in keeping your desires within your current vibration, i.e., your Vibrational Bubble.

In the next few pages I'll explain how affirmations may or may not be helping you include your desire in your Vibrational Bubble and I'll give you a great tool that can help you reword your affirmations so they DO work. Also, I'll introduce you to another tool I call the "Desire Statement." This effective tool ensures that you are including and keeping your new desire in your Vibrational Bubble. It is especially useful when dealing with new desires that may be forgotten if not given deliberate attention.

First let me explain why using affirmations may not be raising your vibration.

Why Using Affirmations May Not Raise Your Vibration

An affirmation is a statement spoken in the present tense and used to declare a desire. Saying "I have a happy, slender body," is an example of a positive affirmation.

Each time you read your affirmation you'll have a reaction based upon how the words make you feel. Remember, the Law Attraction responds to the vibrations you send out based on h you feel, not based on specific words you use. If, for example, you tell yourself that you have a happy, slender body when yo do not, or when having a happy, slender body feels unattainab you'll create negative vibrations. You'll send out a vibration of doubt (a negative vibration), which the Law of Attraction will respond to by giving you more of the same, even though it's unwanted.

A positive affirmation can have a negative vibration. Most affirmations don't work because the Law of Attraction doesn't respond to words – it responds to how you feel about the wor you use.

On the following page you'll see a list of positive affirmations.

After reading each statement, ask yourself which vibration you are sending, negative or positive.

+	−	Vibration
☐	☐	All my family relationships are harmonious
☐	☐	I love my body
☐	☐	I'm a millionaire
☐	☐	My business is booming
☐	☐	I have ideal health
☐	☐	I have a perfect life mate

Question: When would these affirmations offer a positive vibration?

Answer: When they are true for you!

When you state something that is *not* true for you, you are offering a negative vibration because the statement activates doubt within you. As you state the affirmation, a part of you says:

- That's not true, my family relationships aren't harmonious
- That's not true, I don't love my body
- That's not true, I'm not a millionaire yet
- That's not true, my business isn't booming
- That's not true, I don't have ideal health
- That's not true, I don't have a perfect life mate

The key to using affirmations is that they need to be true for you in order to make you feel good. On the following page I'll give you a tool to help you reword an affirmation so it is ALWAYS true for you, thus enabling you to send out a positive vibration.

The Law of Attraction responds to how you feel about what you say and how you feel about what you think.

ool #1: Rewording Your Affirmations o Make Them Feel Better

Some of you have been taught to always state your affirmations in the current tense. Here, I'm suggesting that you are *in the process*. "The process" (the process of manifestation), actually starts when you think about your desire, talk about it, write about it, or when you give it ANY kind of attention, energy and focus. So the truth is you ARE in the process. When you say "I'm in the process of…," that sentence becomes true and if it's true for you, it feels good, which is a positive vibration.

Let's revisit the statements on the previous page, starting each sentence with the following:

I'm in the process of…

♦ I'm in the process of creating ideal family relationships
♦ I'm in the process of enjoying my body more and more
♦ I'm in the process of becoming more abundant
♦ I'm in the process of growing my business
♦ I'm in the process of having ideal health
♦ I'm in the process of attracting an ideal mate

Now each statement is true for you! When a statement is true for you it feels good. When it feels good, you are sending a positive vibration which the Law of Attraction responds to by bringing you more of the same.

Tool #2: The Desire Statement Tool

A Desire Statement is an effective tool for raising your vibration and is the second step in the 3-step process of Deliberate Attraction. Once you're clear about what you want, writing a Desire Statement helps you give attention to that desire. Remember, the Law of Attraction states whatever you give your attention, energy and focus to you'll get more of, and the Desire Statement lets you do just that.

For example, you might say "I want to own my own home." In that moment, the Law of Attraction is orchestrating circumstances and events to bring it to you. However, if you're like most people, you'll probably sabotage yourself by saying you can't afford your own home. Now you're offering a vibration of lack and that's what the Law of Attraction is responding to.

Once you've written your Desire Statement, you will experience feelings of excitement, possibility and hope, all of which are a sign that your vibration has been raised – you can tell by how you feel.

There are three elements to the Desire Statement:

◆ The opening sentence
◆ The body (your Clarity list from Step 1)
◆ The closing sentence

In the following section you'll learn how to use these three elements to create your Desire Statement.

Desire Statement - Opening sentence

I am in the process of attracting all that I need to do, know, or have, to attract my ideal desire.

Desire Statement - Body

Using the statements from your Clarity list, combine them with these phrases:

I love knowing that my ideal _____

I love how it feels when _____

I've decided _____

More and more _____

It excites me _____

I love the idea of _____

I'm excited at the thought of _____

I love seeing myself _____

Examples:

◆ I love knowing that my ideal partner lives in my city.
◆ I love how it feels when I'm doing a bank deposit for my business.
◆ I'm excited at the thought of traveling with my ideal mate.
◆ I love the idea of having a full client base.
◆ I love seeing myself making healthy food choices.

The above phrases allow you to talk about your desire and at the same time knowing it is true for you. You DO love knowing, or love the thought of, or love seeing yourself, etc.. Now you are including a positive vibration about your desire and including it in your Vibrational Bubble. Using the word *ideal* is important here. Referring to an ideal mate, or ideal health, or ideal career, allows you to talk about it *now*, thus enabling you to include it in your current vibration. Remember, the purpose of the Desire Statement is to help you include your new desire in your Vibrational Bubble.

Can you feel the difference in vibration between:

I love knowing that my *ideal* relationship is nurturing and uplifting.

AND

My relationships are nurturing and uplifting.

In the first statement you're saying that your *ideal* relationship nurturing and uplifting and this applies whether you're in one not. Your vibration is positive. Again, you aren't stating that y have your *ideal* relationship right now, but you are saying that you are clear about desiring these attributes that make up you *ideal* relationship.

The second statement is an assertion that you already have nurturing and uplifting relationships. If that isn't true for you, you'll have doubt, which generates a negative vibration.

Desire Statement - Closing sentence

The Law of Attraction is unfolding and orchestrating all that needs to happen to bring me my desire.

Examples of Completed Desire Statements

Before you write your own Desire Statement, let's look at the examples for Janice and Greg. Remember, Janice and Greg's first step was to build a list of contrast (dislikes), to help them become clear about their desires. I've included their Clarity Through Contrast Worksheets here to help show how it helpe them create their Desire Statement.

Clarity Through Contrast Worksheet
Janice
My Ideal Relationship

So, what do I want?

Contrast – *things I don't like* (Side A)	Clarity – *things I like* (Side B)
1. ~~Controlling~~	1. Flexible, well-balanced
2. ~~Poor listener~~	2. Great listening skills
3. ~~Not affectionate~~	3. Affectionate, sensitive
4. ~~Doesn't care what I think or how I feel~~	4. Asks me what I think and how I feel about things
5. ~~Not outgoing~~	5. He likes to meet my friends and enjoys them
6. ~~Doesn't like traveling~~	6. Enjoys social situations. Loves short-term and long-term travel, likes adventure and exploring new places together
7. ~~Always rushes me~~	7. Has patience; allows things to unfold in due time
8. ~~Makes decisions without me~~	8. Asks for my ideas in decision making
9. ~~Doesn't like movies or dancing~~	9. Enjoys theater, movies, loves live bands and entertainment; likes dancing

build her Desire Statement, Janice took her Clarity list and plugged it
the Desire Statement model.

Janice's Desire Statement
My Ideal Relationship

Opening sentence

I am in the process of attracting all that I need to do, know or have to attract my ideal relationship.

Body

I love how it feels knowing that my ideal relationship is with a man who is flexible and well-balanced. He has great listening skills and enjoys conversations.

I love how it feels knowing that my ideal partner is affectionat and sensitive and asks about my feelings. I love being asked to included in decision-making opportunities.

I love knowing that my ideal partner enjoys and looks forward meeting my friends in social situations. My partner and I enjo short-term and long-term travel together, experiencing trips ar vacations that bring us closer.

I've decided that my ideal partner is patient, caring, gentle and allows things to unfold in due time. It feels great to be asked b my ideal partner what I think and feel about things and to ha balanced conversations where each of us is included. I love ask my partner for input and I love being asked.

I'm excited at the thought of enjoying the theatre, movies, live entertainment and dancing with my ideal partner. I love being adored by my ideal partner and I love that my ideal partner enjoys being adored. He is optimistic and loves being uplifted. He's supportive and supportable.

Closing sentence

The Law of Attraction is unfolding and orchestrating all that needs to happen to bring me my desire.

Clarity Through Contrast Worksheet
Greg
My Ideal Financial Situation

So, what do I want?

Contrast – *things I don't like* (Side A)	Clarity – *things I like* (Side B)
~~Not enough money~~	1. Abundance of money
~~Always bills to pay~~	2. Bills are paid easily and quickly
~~Just making ends meet~~	3. Always have excess money
~~I can't afford anything I want~~	4. Always have enough money to purchase whatever I desire
~~Money flow is sporadic~~	5. Constant flow of money is coming in from multiple sources
~~I never win anything~~	6. I win prizes often; receive gifts and many free things
~~I'll always make the same amount of money~~	7. I am constantly increasing my amount of monetary intake from known and unknown sources
~~Money does not come easily in my family~~	8. Money comes easily to me
~~I always struggle to pay the rent~~	9. Rent is paid easily as I always have money
~~Money issues stress me~~	10. Money and my relationship with it feels good

Greg's Desire Statement
My Ideal Financial Situation

Opening sentence

I am in the process of attracting all that I need to do, know or have to attract my ideal financial situation.

Body

I love knowing that my ideal financial situation allows me to have and enjoy everything that I need and desire to bring more joy and freedom to my life.

Abundance is a feeling and I love the feeling of abundance all around me. I love knowing that all my bills are paid with joy, knowing that what I am billed for is an exchange, using money to honor that exchange.

I'm so excited at the thought of a constant flow of money coming to me from known and unknown sources.

I love knowing that my ideal financial situation brings me the comfort and the knowledge that I can travel where I want, shop where I want, and have whatever will make me feel great.

More and more, I receive gifts, win more prizes, and receive what I need from unknown and known sources.

I love the thought of stashing money away into excellent investments.

Closing sentence

The Law of Attraction is unfolding and orchestrating all that needs to happen to bring me my desire.

w to Create Your Desire Statement

Now it's your turn to create your own Desire Statement.

Use the items on your completed Clarity Through Contrast Worksheet to build the body of your Desire Statement on the following worksheet.

I have provided you with the opening and closing sentences. All you have to do is fill in the body.

Use some or all of the following phrases to help describe your ideal desire:

I love knowing that my ideal _____

I love how it feels when _____

I've decided _____

More and more _____

It excites me _____

I love the idea of _____

I'm excited at the thought of _____

I love seeing myself _____

There are two blank worksheets on the following pages. For more copies, go to www.LawofAttractionBook.com/worksheets.html

Desire Statement Worksheet

Desire Statement
My Ideal _____

I am in the process of attracting all that I need to do, know or have to attract my ideal

_____

_____

_____

_____

_____

_____

_____

_____

_____

_____

_____

The Law of Attraction is unfolding and orchestrating all that needs to happen to bring me my desire.

Desire Statement Worksheet

Desire Statement
My Ideal _____

I am in the process of attracting all that I need to do, know or have to attract my ideal

_____

_____

_____

_____

_____

_____

_____

_____

_____

_____

The Law of Attraction is unfolding and orchestrating all that needs to happen to bring me my desire.

How Do I Know If I'm Doing It Right?

After you've written your Desire Statement, go back and read it. Next, ask yourself how you feel. Do you hear a little negative voice or have an uncomfortable feeling? Does your Desire Statement make you feel great? If not, then revise your statement so that you feel better (raise your vibration) when you read it. Remember, the purpose of the Desire Statement is to raise your vibration to help you include your new desire in your Vibration Bubble.

Wrapping up Step 2:
Give Your Desire Attention

You have completed the second phase of Deliberate Attraction: Giving your desire attention.

Here's what we've covered in this section

◆ Your Vibrational Bubble contains all of your current vibrations.

◆ You must include the vibration of your new desire in your current Vibrational Bubble.

◆ A Desire Statement helps you include the vibration of your desire in your Vibrational Bubble.

◆ The purpose of Step 2 is to give your desire attention.

◆ You raise your vibration when you give your desire attention, energy and focus.

◆ Your affirmations may not feel good when the statements aren't true for you.

◆ Law of Attraction responds to how you feel about your affirmations.

Now that you've completed Step 1 and Step 2 of the Law of Attraction formula, it's time to apply the third step – Allowing

ep 3 - Allow It

s All About Allowing

Now some of you may be saying "I've had desires in the past that I got excited about and they never resulted in anything." Remember, Deliberate Attraction is a 3-step process.

You've identified your desire and given it your attention. The third step in the Deliberate Attraction process is 'Allowing'. Let's get started.

Allowing is simply the absence of negative vibration and doubt is a negative vibration. Allowing is the most important step in the Deliberate Attraction process. One of my clients, Danny, asked me why he did not attract his desires. He had built a great Clarity list of his ideal clients and made an awesome Desire Statement that felt great. So why didn't he attract his desires?

The process didn't work for him because it was not enough for him to just identify his desire and really want it. He also had to remove any doubt surrounding his belief that he would attract it. This doubt-removing process is called Allowing.

You may have heard the expression "Just allow it." Telling yourself this doesn't help you to allow. If you doubt you can have something, you are sending a negative vibration. This negative vibration is diluting or cancelling the positive vibration of your desire. In other words, having strong desire (positive vibe), and having strong doubt (negative vibe), cancel each other out. Therefore, Allowing occurs in the absence of doubt.

Allowing is the absence of negative vibration (doubt).

You know you are Allowing something when you hear yourself saying statements such as:

◆ "Ah, what a relief!"
◆ "You know, maybe I can have this."
◆ "Now this feels possible."

In all three of the above expressions, what you are actually describing is the feeling of the negative vibration being removed.

Most people say that Allowing is the most difficult step in the Law of Attraction formula. It's not the most difficult step; it's just the least understood. Most people don't understand how to allow so they become frustrated when people say "Just allow it."

In this section, I'll give you *how-to tools* to help you allow.

The Allowing Game

Here is a model to help you understand the importance of Allowing, as illustrated by a simple children's game.

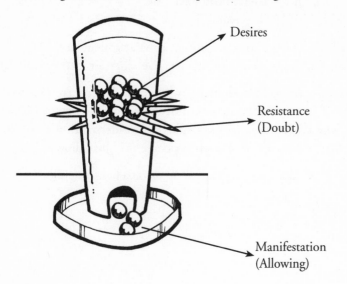

Desires

Resistance (Doubt)

Manifestation (Allowing)

Here's how the game works. A number of marbles rest on stic that criss-cross through a clear cylinder. The sticks represent resistance/doubt, the marbles represent desire, and the fallen marbles represent manifestation (Allowing).

In the course of the game, the sticks are removed allowing sor marbles to fall to the bottom of the cylinder.

As you can see in the diagram, the only way the marbles will fall is if the sticks are removed. In the same way, having a strong desire is not enough – it is only when your resistance is removed that your desire is manifested. The faster your resistance/doubt is removed, the faster your desire can be realized.

In other words, the speed at which the Law of Attraction manifests your desire is in direct proportion to how much you are Allowing.

Here are a couple of questions to ponder:

Does having strong desire make your desire manifest faster?
Do you have to remove all your doubt to manifest your desire?

The following illustrations will answer these questions.

In other words, the speed at which the Law of Attraction responds to your desire is in direct proportion to how much you allow.

The Power of Allowing

Having a strong desire with strong doubt means your desire will not be manifested.

Having a strong desire with just a little bit of doubt means your desire will come, though slowly.

Having a strong desire with no doubt means your desire will be manifested quickly.

Although smiling, these lottery ticket purchasers have thoughts of doubt about winning.

If you have a strong desire and strong doubt, your desire will come slowly to you, if at all. The speed at which you'll win the lottery (your desire) is determined by how much doubt you have. Do you have doubts?

The speed at which Law of Attraction manifests your desire is in direct proportion to how much you Allow.

...ere Does Doubt Come From?

The most common source of doubt (negative vibration) is from your own limiting beliefs.

What is a Limiting Belief?

A limiting belief is a repetitive thought that you think over and over, and over again. When your thoughts consist of a limiting belief you are offering or sending out a negative vibration. That negative vibration is preventing you from attracting your desire. The phrase "I have to work hard to make money" vibrates lack, which stops you from getting what you want.

How Can You Identify Your Limiting Beliefs?

Here's an easy way to identify your limiting beliefs. They are usually found after you say the word *because*, as in the phrase, "*I can't because...*"

Here are some examples:

- I'd like to write a book but I can't *because* I don't have a university degree.
- I'd like to start my own business but I can't *because* I'm too old.
- I'd like to have a more slender body but it's so hard *because* everybody in my family is overweight.
- I'd like to have an ideal mate but I can't *because* I'm too fat, too old or too shy, etc.

Let's go back to our two case studies with Janice and Greg. Janice's desire was to attract her ideal relationship. She caught herself saying that she couldn't attract an ideal partner *because* she was too old. And Greg caught himself saying that he couldn't be financially wealthy *because* he comes from a poor family.

So what are your limiting beliefs? When you catch yourself saying the word *because*, you've just discovered one of your limiting beliefs.

In this section, you'll learn how to use tools that will assist you in changing your limiting beliefs.

*Allowing is the absence
of negative vibration.
Doubt is a negative vibration
and doubt
is often created from
limiting beliefs.*

ol to Help You Allow

There are a number of tools for Allowing. The first one we're going to explore is Allowing Statements. The purpose of Allowing Statements is to lessen or remove any doubt that is preventing you from receiving what you want. After making your Allowing Statements you will experience a feeling of relief. That is, you will believe that you really are going to attract what you desire. Believing is also the absence of doubt, as is faith.

Two Ways to Know You've Allowed

Remembering that Allowing is the absence of negative vibration, there are two ways you can tell if you are allowing:

◆ First, you can tell by how you feel. When you remove a negative feeling of resistance, most people feel a sense of relief or hear themselves saying "Ah, this feels much better!"

◆ The second way that you can tell is by noticing when manifestation appears in your life. When evidence is showing up in your life, you know you are allowing.

In the following pages you'll learn how to change your thoughts to positive ones. Offering these new positive thoughts over and over again will then create your new beliefs. Remember, a limiting belief is simply a repetitive thought you think over and over again, therefore, any belief can be changed.

Formula for Creating Allowing Statements

Whenever you hear yourself stating a limiting belief (or having doubt), you can use this formula to help create an Allowing Statement which will help lessen or remove your doubt.

Writing your own Allowing Statements is simple.

◆ Start by asking yourself if there is anyone currently doing what you want to do or having what you want?
◆ If so, then how many people have been doing this today? Yesterday? Last week? Last month? Last year?
◆ Write your statements in general terms (3rd person), because making reference to yourself may create more doubt.
◆ Ensure that the statements are plausible.

Here is an example of how to create Allowing Statements for the following limiting beliefs.

Limiting Belief #1:

I'd like to have a more slender body but I can't because all my family members are big.

Question: Is there anyone on the planet who has a different body size than other members of their family?
Answer: Yes

Question: If so, how many people have this today? Yesterday? Last week? Last month? Last year?

Allowing Statement:

Thousands of people, even in my neighbourhood, have different body sizes than their family members. There are millions of men on the planet that have a more slender body than their father or brother. (Note: This sentence is written in general terms, in the 3rd person, to exclude making any reference to yourself.)

Limiting Belief #2:

I'd like to start my own business but I can't because I'm 50 years old!

Question: Is there anyone my age on the planet that has started their own business?

Answer: Yes

Question: If so, then how many people have been doing this today? Yesterday? Last week? Last month? Last year?

Allowing Statement:

Right now there are hundreds of people in their fifties who are starting and running successful businesses. There are millions of 50-year-old (plus) successful business owners.

Write your Allowing Statements in general terms (3rd person), because making reference to yourself may create more doubt.

Now, let's return to Janice and Greg to see how they created their Allowing Statements.

As you'll recall, Janice is tired and frustrated because she continually has the wrong kind of man showing interest in her. She complains that she attracts men who are unavailable, insensitive and who never make her a priority.

Janice is using Deliberate Attraction to help her attract her ideal relationship. She is clear about her desires and is already using a Desire Statement. Because this is a new desire for her, she has to lessen the doubt in order to receive it. She does this by composing Allowing Statements.

Janice's Allowing Statements
My Ideal Relationship

- Hundreds of people met their ideal partner last month.
- Thousands of people are on first dates today with a perso
  who will become their lifelong ideal partner.
- Hundreds of thousands of couples are enjoying each othe
  company today.
- Millions of couples are in their ideal relationship.
- Every day more and more people are attracting their idea
  partners.
- Millions of couples are doing social activities together tha
  include travelling and vacations.
- Hundreds of thousands of couples will go dancing this we

As Janice reads her Allowing Statements, she begins to feel ho
and the reduction of doubt. Now, the Law of Attraction can
bring Janice her ideal mate.

Remember Greg? He's the self-employed consultant and business advisor who's having a really hard time making ends meet. He constantly complains about not having enough money. In fact, he says he's feeling pretty stressed out about his financial situation.

Greg is using Deliberate Attraction to help him attract his ideal financial situation. He is clear about his desires and is already using a Desire Statement. Because this is a new desire for him, he has to lessen and remove the doubt in order to manifest. He does this by composing Allowing Statements.

Greg's Allowing Statements
My Ideal Financial Situation

◆ Millions of people are receiving checks today.
◆ Every day, billions of dollars are moved from bank account to bank account.
◆ Someone just received a check this minute.
◆ Hundreds of thousands of people win prizes and money every day.
◆ Somebody became a millionaire yesterday.
◆ Millions of dollars are inherited every day.
◆ Someone found money today.
◆ More and more people are attracting creative ways to bring in extra income.

As Greg reads his Allowing Statements he begins to feel hope and the diminishing of doubt. Now the Law of Attraction can respond to Greg's desire for his ideal financial situation.

How to Create Your Own Allowing Statement

It's time for you to create your own Allowing Statement. The Allowing Statement is used when you hear yourself make statements of doubt. Build a list of these doubts. You may he yourself saying "I can't have that *because*…," or "That won't happen to me *because*…!" You can use the Allowing Stateme worksheet on the next page to help build your Allowing Statements.

1st STEP: Uncover the Doubt

Reread your Desire Statement and use it to uncover any doub you feel as a result of reading it. For example, if your desire statement says that your ideal job allows you to work a 4-day week and you hear a little voice inside you saying "That will never happen because…," then jot down your doubt.

2nd STEP: Ask Yourself These Questions

Start by asking yourself whether there is anyone currently doi what you want to do or having what you want to have. If so, then how many people have been doing this today? Yesterday Last week? Last month? Last year?

3rd STEP: Write in General Terms (in the 3rd person)

Write your statements in general terms because making refere to yourself often creates more doubt. Ensure that the stateme are plausible.

Allowing Statements
My Ideal _____

_____

_____

_____

_____

_____

_____

_____

_____

_____

_____

_____

_____

_____

For more copies of this worksheet, go to
www.LawofAttractionBook.com/worksheets.html

There are two ways to tell when you are Allowing.

First, you feel a sense of relief and often hear yourself saying "Ah! This feels much better."

Second, you see evidence of your manifestation appearing in your life.

ore Tools to Help You Allow

n addition to the Allowing Statement Tool, here are additional
ools.

1. Celebrate the Proof (Evidence)
2. Record Your Proof of the Law of Attraction
3. Appreciation and Gratitude
4. Use the Expression, "I'm in the Process of…"
5. Use the Expression, "I've Decided…"
6. Use the Expression, "Lots Can Happen…"
7. Ask for Information
8. Make Yourself an Attraction Box
9. Create a Void or Vacuum
10. Allow the Law of Attraction to figure it out

Remember, it's the absence of doubt that will bring your desire faster.

Tool #1: Celebrate the Proof (Evidence)

Remember that to manifest your desire you need to remove the doubt. Doubt is what stops your desire from coming to you. The best way to remove doubt is to find proof. Scientists, for example, only believe something after it's been proven. Like most of us, when someone proves something to us, we often say "Okay, I believe it now. I can see the proof." Here's how to use proof (evidence) to your advantage.

Have you noticed when something you desire starts showing up in your life, even just a little bit, it excites you? For example, you attract a bit of information you've been looking for, or you meet someone who is a pretty close match to your ideal partner or your ideal client. All of this is proof (evidence) of the Law of Attraction at work in your life.

How you observe proof (evidence) of the Law of Attraction is important. In some cases, people might say "Oh, this isn't exactly what I want," or "He's not quite the right person I was looking for," or "It's kind of close but not really." Saying or thinking these kinds of phrases creates a negative vibration.

When you find and experience proof (evidence) of the Law of Attraction, celebrate it by acknowledging how close you came to getting what you desired. It's in the celebration of the closeness of the match that you offer more vibration of what you desire, and at that moment, the Law of Attraction is responding to your vibration. Remember, the Law of Attraction does not care whether you are remembering, pretending, playing, creating, complaining or worrying. It simply responds to your vibration and sends you more of the same. So find proof and rejoice.

Janice, who is using the Law of Attraction to attract her ideal relationship, is a great example of how this tool can be used to lessen doubt.

Shortly after Janice completed her Desire Statement and started using the Allowing tools, she met a man who was a visitor to her city. They hit it off right away. They had lots in common including a love of music, theatre, and movies. She was really impressed by his good communication skills and how upbeat he was. Three days later, Janice called me and I could hear some disappointment in her voice. She spent lots of time and attention describing her disappointment that he was from another country (thus, including what she didn't want in her Vibrational Bubble). Yet I knew he was a close match to her desire and that she was not acknowledging that fact. My job was to help her include all those things that were a match in her Vibrational Bubble.

Here's how I used this tool with Janice. I simply asked her to tell me all the things about her new relationship that excited her. In other words, the things that were in her Desire Statement that made her feel great. She quickly built a list that included his great communication skills; his love of music, theatre, and movies; his values; and how happy she felt around him. Janice could feel her vibration rise the moment she started creating this list. Finding and celebrating the closeness of the match shifted her vibration immediately. As Janice began recalling and noticing the closeness of the match she was once again including this vibration in her Vibrational Bubble.

And you know how the Law of Attraction responds to that!

Tool #2: Record Proof of the Law of Attraction

Keeping a diary or a Book of Proof of the Law of Attraction in your life will help you believe it more, get excited more, allow more, and trust more. Regardless of the size of the manifestation (e.g., you found a quarter or you won a prize), if it's something you desired – log it! Record your proof and you will raise your vibration.

Finding proof helps lessens doubt. Remember that any time you've ever had something proven to you, in that very moment, all doubt is removed. You might have heard yourself saying "NOW I believe that!"

After a couple of pages of recording proof you will realize how much the Law of Attraction is really working in your life. As you use the Law of Attraction more knowingly, you will have confirmation that will help you trust the process of Allowing more easily, thus lessening the doubt (resistance). Remember, it's the absence of doubt that will bring your desire faster.

So whenever you're feeling doubtful about the Law of Attraction, you just need to read your Book of Proof. Reading your Book of Proof will remind you of the evidence you've received and will lower or remove your doubt.

Example of a Book of Proof

Date: _____
Today I observed this proof (evidence)

Money left in parking meter	Free parking validation ticket
I was treated to lunch today	Free sample at coffee shop
Got 30% off a purchase	Was given free advice over dinner

Book of Proof

Date: _____
Today I observed this proof (evidence)

Date: _____
Today I observed this proof (evidence)

Date: _____
Today I observed this proof (evidence)

For more copies of this worksheet, go to
www.LawofAttractionBook.com/worksheets.html

The Book of Proof Worked for Ivor

Being analytically minded (I work in the financial business), I figured I was the most unlikely person to get involved with the Law of Attraction. But through Michael's teachings, I learned how to change my thoughts and be open and receptive to new ideas. Then wonderful things began to happen. I started taking an optimistic approach to business situations that I would generally worry about. When I deliberately raised my vibration from worry to a positive, happy mood, I noticed that I got results – and they came fast. If I decided I wanted to meet three new clients in one day, that's what happened! One of the ways I log proof of how the Law of Attraction is working for me is I use my Book of Proof to record all my successes, both big and small. I record when I am successful in getting a referral, a new client, paying off a bill or receiving a big check, etc. I refer to my book often – whenever I want to raise my vibration and remind myself how powerful the Law of Attraction is.

Ivor John
Financial Advisor
Victoria, BC

Remember, the Law of Attraction does not care whether you are remembering, pretending, celebrating, playing, creating, complaining or worrying.

It simply responds to what's in your Vibrational Bubble.

So, find proof, rejoice and send out a positive vibration.

Tool #3: Appreciation and Gratitude

Appreciation and gratitude help you send out strong positive vibrations. When you're appreciating something, you're offering a feeling and vibration of pure joy. Think of a time when you expressed thanks for someone in your life. The feelings you experienced were positive.

Keeping an appreciation and gratitude journal is an effective daily tool for maintaining a positive vibration. When you purposely take time to appreciate every day you are intentionally offering strong, positive vibrations, and including those vibrations in your Vibrational Bubble.

You can take time to appreciate anything. It's the feeling that's attached to your appreciation that is important.

Janice, whose desire is an ideal relationship, keeps a daily appreciation journal. It allows her to reflect on the relationships that she loves in her life. Here are a few samples of Janice's appreciation statements:

- ◆ I am grateful that I went hiking with new friends this week.
- ◆ I loved sharing lunch today with close friends.
- ◆ I appreciate my close friends giving me their attention.
- ◆ I love having lots of friends.

While Janice is thinking and writing her daily appreciation statements, she is offering a positive vibration. In that same moment the Law of Attraction is unfolding to bring her more of what she is offering 'vibrationally.'

Take time to appreciate anything. It's the feeling that's attached to your appreciation that is important. Appreciation and gratitude help you offer strong, positive vibrations.

Tool #4: Use the Expression, "I'm in the Process of..."

Sometimes it's hard to believe you will get what you desire. This is especially true if you're focusing on the fact that you haven't reached your goal. When you concentrate on what you don't have, you're offering a negative vibration. So instead, feel the relief by saying "I'm in the process of..."

Saying you don't have something is another way of focusing on your lack and generates a negative vibration. When you catch yourself saying you don't have something yet, stop, and instead say "I'm in the process of attracting..."

Some people may ask "Then are you not always in the process of?" The answer is yes, you are always *in the process of.* The Law of Attraction is always unfolding and orchestrating events and circumstances to respond to your vibration and bring you more of the same. As you attract whatever it is you've desired, once it manifests, you'll generate a new desire and once again be *in the process of.*

In the very moment you think about a new desire, talk about it, write about it, put it on your calendar, or on a reminder note on your fridge, you have just begun *the process of* because in each of these cases, you are giving your new desire attention, energy and focus. So it is true...you are *in the process of!*

Here are some examples of how to apply the tool "I'm in the process of..."

Before: I still haven't attracted my ideal mate.
 ◆ I'm in the process of attracting my ideal mate.

Before: I'm still waiting for my ideal job.
 ◆ I'm in the process of obtaining my ideal job.

Before: I haven't reached my goal weight yet.
 ◆ I'm in the process of having a happier, slender body.

Remember to use this expression whenever you're focusing on the doubt of not reaching your goals or manifesting your desires.

Tool #5: Use the Expression, "I've Decided..."

Another way to rephrase your expressions so they offer a posi‑
vibration is to use the phrase "I've decided." Have you notice
that in most cases when you say "I've decided..." it creates a
strong positive emotion. "I've decided I'm having this," or "I'
decided I'm doing that." Most people rarely use the word *dec*
yet it is an excellent way to take your focus off of lack and pu
back onto your desire.

- ◆ I've decided I'm going to have more money in my life
- ◆ I've decided I'm going to work three days a week.
- ◆ I've decided I'm going to be in a happy, healthy
   relationship.
- ◆ I've decided to start my own business.
- ◆ I've decided to attract my ideal job.

You may have noticed that when some people experience con
they may declare loudly "That's enough! I've decided from no
on I'm having it this way!" So deciding is really about making
a decision and with that decision you send out the vibration o
what you want to attract.

Decide more often. You'll feel instant relief from the positive
emotions that come with each act of deciding.

Tool #6: Use the Expression, "Lots Can Happen..."

I had a client, Jason, who was using the Law of Attraction to attract his ideal customer. I could hear in his words that he was trying to determine where his next major purchaser was coming from. He was saying things like "It seems like I've been waiting forever. I wonder when this is going to happen?" Even though Jason had completed the entire 3-step process, there was still a part of him that doubted. The statements Jason was making about his next client had a negative vibration of lack (doubt).

Jason was spending a lot of energy trying to figure out why he wasn't getting what he wanted and was noticing that he wasn't reaching his goals. Like Jason, you've probably spent some time noticing you haven't reached your goals.

Here are some questions that I asked Jason to help him go from his place of not reaching his goals to a place of possibility.

- ◆ Can lots happen in the next few days?
- ◆ Can lots happen in the next week?
- ◆ Can lots happen in the next 30 days?

Jason excitedly answered "Yes" to all of these questions. The moment I reminded Jason about the phrase "Lots can happen," I could see his relief. This experience also reminded him of times when lots happened even when he doubted lots could happen. Using this Allowing phrase helped Jason shift his vibration from lack to abundance, or from a negative vibration to a positive one.

From now on, the moment you notice a lack of results, focus on the possibility that "lots can happen."

Tool #7: Ask for Information

Often when we define our desires and get excited about attract
them, the doubt we may have stops the Law of Attraction from
bringing them to us. If your desire is to have a full client base,
example, you may doubt that it is possible. However, you coul
desire to attract information that will help you with that goal.
Try it. If you feel more hopeful after you've asked for informati
then you just reduced your doubts, which allows the Law of
Attraction to bring your desires to you more quickly.

Example: I'd like to attract some more information on where
get started with my new desire.

- I'd like to start attracting information about my desire
  to get me started.
- I'd like the LAW OF ATTRACTION to bring to
  me some creative information on how I can manifest
  my desire.
- I'd like to attract some information and ideas about
  more ways to generate business.
- I'd like some information about where to network
  my new business.

We have less resistance to accepting information and as a resu
information comes quickly because there is no negative vibra
to stop it from coming.

One of the best techniques for breaking things down is the on
I used with Greg's financial situation. Even after completing t
3-step process, he still felt doubtful that he could have what
he desired.

I asked Greg just to take the first step. That is, to ask for and
accept any information that fit with his desire to receive more
money. Greg instantly got excited and said "Oh, what a great
start! I can attract information about what I need to do to
attract more money. That's what I need. Now THAT I can do

Tool #8: Make Yourself an Attraction Box

An Attraction Box is used to collect things that represent your desire: things you've cut out of magazines and newspapers, brochures for trips you want to take, or even business cards of people you want to work with.

Your Attraction Box can be any type of container, as simple as a shoebox, or as elaborate as a treasure chest.

Each time you put something into your Attraction Box, what you are actually offering 'vibrationally' is hope, and hope is a positive vibration. Instead of throwing out the catalogues and the flyers and saying things like "I can't afford this," or "I'll never be able to have one of these," you now allow it. You do this because it's not your job to figure out where or when your desire is going to come. Just put it into your Attraction Box and leave the rest to the Law of Attraction.

Tool #9: Create a Void or Vacuum

A void or vacuum is always waiting to be filled.

As an example let's say you're looking for more clients. By making space in your filing cabinet for new clients, even by labelling some empty file folders with the words "Next new client," it does two things – it sets the intention that you wa to attract new clients and it also creates a void to be filled. Sa "I'm waiting for new clients," or "I have only a few clients," be rephrased as "I have room and space for new clientele." D you hear how optimistic that sounds? Does it feel better?

Some voids can be created intentionally. For example, go to y daytimer and enter this on your calendar, "New client here," or "New appointment goes here," or "Sales happen here." N you've created the void and intention to attract those things. When you look at your calendar you'll be reminded of your intention of what you want to attract in those time slots, thu giving it more attention, energy and focus.

The other kind of void is unintentional. It's when a client cancels. When a client cancels, most people will complain or worry about the cancellation, spending too much time focusi on the cancellation and giving it negative attention. You can change the vibration by saying "I've just created a void to att a new client," or "I've just created some more room for anotl project in my business."

Now, that's Allowing!

Tool #10: Allow the Law of Attraction to Figure It Out

Sometimes it can get a little overwhelming thinking about your desire and all that you need to do to obtain it. You needn't be overwhelmed because the Law of Attraction will bring the results to you.

At the very moment that you catch yourself saying:

- I don't know how to figure this out.
- I don't know where to look.
- I don't know how to find this information.
- I don't know what to do next.
- I'm having problems finding this.
- I can't figure it out.

Stop! Say to yourself "That's not my job. I'm going to allow the Law of Attraction to figure this out."

This lesson was a valuable one for my client and friend Andria. When she was first going into business for herself, she used the Law of Attraction to attract her ideal business. Using the 3-step process, Andria discovered a business that really got her excited by allowing her to shop every day. She also used the Law of Attraction to find financing and the perfect location for her clothing consignment store. Every step of the way, whenever any tough questions came up and Andria would worry about the details, I would say to her "That's not your job. Let the Law of Attraction figure it out."

Although the Law of Attraction took care of the big questions, Andria still had to do the follow-up actions. For example, after she found the name of the perfect banker, she still had to make an appointment to see him and arrange financing for her shop.

There comes a time when you need to take action. As you let the Law of Attraction figure it out and you start to receive things that are in alignment with your desire, you can then decide when to take action.

Your job is not to try to figure things out intellectually but to let the Law of Attraction figure it out.

Wrapping Up Step 3: Allowing

You have completed the 3rd step of Deliberate Attraction –
Allowing.

Here's what we've covered in this section

♦ Allowing – the 3rd step of the Deliberate Attraction
  process is the most important step
♦ Allowing is the absence of doubt
♦ Doubt is a negative vibration
♦ The negative vibration of doubt cancels
  the positive vibration of a desire
♦ A limiting belief is a repetitive thought
♦ When you say " I can't because…," you've just uncovered
  a limiting belief
♦ Finding proof helps you remove doubt
♦ Finding evidence that others are having or doing what
  you want to have or do helps remove your doubt
♦ The purpose of Allowing tools is to help you remove
  doubt
♦ **10 Allowing Tools:**
  - Celebrate the Evidence of Proof
  - Record Proof of the Law of Attraction
  - Appreciation and Gratitude
  - Use the Expression, "I'm in the Process of…"
  - Use the Expression, "I've Decided…"
  - Use the Expression, "Lots Can Happen…"
  - Ask for Information
  - Make Yourself an Attraction Box
  - Create a Void or Vacuum
  - Allow the Law of Attraction to Figure It Out

Putting It All Together

Now that you've learned how to use the Law of Attraction to get more of what you want and less of what you don't want, you can start using the tools from this book right away.

The worksheets for Step 1, 2 and 3 plus bonus worksheets are available online for free.

Visit: www.LawofAttractionBook.com/worksheets.html

eyond the 3-Step Formula

- **Become More Abundant and Attract More Money**

- **Relationships and Your Vibration**

- **Parents and Teachers: Learn How to Teach Law of Attraction to Children**

Abundance is a feeling. Be more deliberate to include the feeling of abundance in your current vibration – your Vibrational Bubble.

ecome More Abundant
d Attract More Money

You have learned so far that all feelings give off vibrations, either positive or negative. Abundance is a feeling and that's GOOD news. Why? All feelings can be duplicated! Abundance is a feeling and that feeling has a corresponding vibration that you can duplicate. In many cases people are duplicating the feeling of lack, sadness or hopelessness simply by the thoughts and the words they use. Given that you can generate feelings by your words and thoughts, you can learn how to duplicate the feelings of abundance more intentionally by changing the way you use your words and thoughts.

Law of Attraction doesn't know if you are generating a thought by remembering, pretending, creating, visualizing or daydreaming. It simply responds to our vibration in that moment, and we can only send out one vibration at a time! By creating the vibration of abundance more deliberately and more often, we are including it in our Vibrational Bubble more often, thus increasing abundance in our life.

Your objective is to include the vibration of abundance in you Vibrational Bubble as often and as long as possible. The good news is it is easy to duplicate the vibration of abundance. You may be abundant in your life every day and haven't noticed it celebrated it, or talked about it, therefore not including it in your Vibrational Bubble.

Build a list of all the sources and resources where money and abundance can come from. Most people when asked "How c you get more money?" answer by saying that they could work more hours to earn more money, or get a part-time job to ear more money. For these people, their belief that this is the onl way to increase their abundance is a limiting belief. There are actually many, many other ways where abundance is evident your life.

On the following page there is a partial list of areas that can be deemed as abundant. In other words, when you experienc anything on the following list, for most people it generates th feeling of abundance within them.

You may also notice that in many cases the feeling of abunda is not always related to money.

rces of Abundance (examples)

- Someone treats you to lunch (or breakfast or dinner)
- Someone gives you free advice or coaching
- You receive gifts
- You receive free transportation or lodging
- You get your 2nd cup of coffee free
- Someone gives you a prize
- You buy something at a discount or on sale
- You get to use air mile points
- You win door prizes
- You trade or exchange with somebody
- You sell your products or services
- (Add more of your own…)

Other Sources of Abundance

_____
_____
_____
_____
_____
_____
_____
_____
_____
_____
_____
_____
_____
_____

Tools for Including the Vibration of Abundance in Your Vibrational Bubble

Tool #1: Record Evidence of Your *Abundant-ness*

Keep a daily log of all the sources from which you are receivin abundance. This will significantly help you in noticing abundance in your life. Keeping a daily log shows you concre proof (evidence) that abundance DOES exist and IS already present in your life. Celebrate! When you notice abundance, celebrate the evidence of it in your life – and while celebrating know that you are offering the positive vibration of abundance Remember – at every moment, including right now, the Law Attraction is responding to the vibration you are offering and giving you more of the same. Keeping this log encourages you to spend more time celebrating your *abundant-ness*, thereby including it in your Vibration Bubble more frequently.

Here is an example of an entry in a Daily Log to track *Abundant-ness*.

I'm Abundant. Today I attracted abundance when:

◆ A friend paid for my lunch.
◆ During lunch I received a half hour of free coaching.
◆ I had free transportation to and from the airport.
◆ I received a check from a client.
◆ I received a thank-you email.
◆ I got a deal on my new eyeglasses.
◆ Others …

Maintain your own daily log. Do this exercise for the next seven days and you will notice yourself saying "I'm so abundant! I've attracted evidence of abundance every day for the last seven days," or "I'm so abundant! I've attracted 100s of dollars of free advice in the last seven days." Ideally, you would continue to do this well beyond seven days.

Become more deliberate in your offering of the vibration of abundance and the Law of Attraction will bring you more of the same.

Use the worksheet on the next page to start logging your evidence of abundance today.

Evidence of Abundance Journal

I'm Abundant. Today I attracted…	Date:

I'm Abundant. Today I attracted…	Date:

I'm Abundant. Today I attracted…	Date:

I'm Abundant. Today I attracted…	Date:

For more copies of this worksheet, go to
www.LawofAttractionBook.com/worksheets.html

Tool #2: Always Say Yes to Money

A lot of people feel challenged to say *yes* when someone offers to pay for their lunch or buy them a gift or wants to simply give them money. Many people when offered to have their lunch paid for respond with "No that's okay, you don't need to do that," or "Oh no, I'll pay for my own. You don't have to buy me lunch," or "Oh no, I couldn't!" Does this sound like you or someone you know?

In all of these statements you can hear resistance to receiving money. The new you, however, will learn to say "Thanks, I would like that," and you'll start to feel good about it. You may experience discomfort at first but as you continue to say *yes*, it will get easier and you will feel your resistance fading away. This in turn opens up your allowing for more money. Start saying yes to money today!

Tool #3: Hold Onto That Check

Do you want to raise your vibration when it comes to receiving more money? Then hang onto checks you've received for a little bit longer.

Instead of cashing a check the day you get it, holding onto it will generate more 'vibrational' value if you observe it for a day or more. Every time you view the check you will get a little jolt of excitement that will be offered to the Law of Attraction.

Remember that each time you feel that little jolt of excitement, you are now including that vibration in your Vibrational Bubble. When you notice that something made you excited about money, do it over and over again. The Law of Attraction is always responding.

Wrapping Up: Abundance and Attracting More Money

Here's what we've covered in this section

◆ Be more deliberate to include the feeling of abundance in your current vibration

◆ Become aware of many different sources of abundance

◆ Recording evidence of abundance increases your attention to the vibration of abundance

◆ Your job is to include the vibration of abundance as often as possible in your Vibrational Bubble

◆ Celebrate the moment you notice you've attracted something abundant

◆ **Three tools to help you attract abundance more deliberately:**

    – Record evidence of your abundant-ness

    – Always say yes to money

    – Hold onto that check

:lationships and Your Vibration

Have you noticed at times when you meet somebody that within seconds you are saying to yourself "I don't like their energy?" At other times, you meet someone and can tell you are hitting it off with them within seconds because you catch yourself saying "I sure like their energy." These kinds of experiences show that you've already been *picking up* other peoples' energy, or vibes.

If we were to measure your vibration on a scale of 1-100, 100 being a very high vibe and 1 being a very low vibe, where would your vibe be?

Imagine a radio dial showing station '0' to station '100'. All the radio stations between 0 to 50 are negative talk-radio and all the stations from 50 to 100 are positive-talk radio.

Your vibes are similar to the vibes of radio frequencies. When you are feeling really good and everything is working out in your life, things come to you easily, and everyone in your life is positive. We could say that your vibe is as high as 98.5 on the radio dial.

How can you tell when you are on 98.5? You can tell by how you feel. You can see by the diagram and by how you are feeling when your vibe is high, that it means there is little to no negative vibration around you. When there is little to no negative vibration around you then everything comes to you much quicker. You start attracting relationships that are of a similar vibration. Some of you may also notice that as you've been moving up the dial (raising your vibration), you start attracting like-minded and like-vibration people in all areas of your life.

The distance between your vibration and someone else's vibration is equal to the amount of resistance (negativity) you feel when you are with them.

On the other hand, many of you may also be familiar with the saying "Negativity breeds negativity." Most of us have people in our lives that aren't on station 98.5 at the same time when we are. Recall a time in your life when your vibration was high. You're having one great experience followed by another and you love everything in your life. Then your telephone rings. You look at the call display and it's somebody in your life that's at a much lower vibration than you. As a matter of fact just seeing their name lowers your vibration. Let's call this person your *Negative-Nelly*.

Your *Negative-Nelly*

Some people may ask "How can I even attract a *Negative-Nelly* if I have such a high vibration?" The answer is simple. You didn't necessarily attract them by choice. The *Negative-Nelly* in your life could be, for example, your partner, workmate, colleague, child, parent or neighbor.

Let's say for example that *Negative-Nelly's* vibration is consistently low, on station 30.1, and your vibration is on 98.5. Looking at the radio station below you can see the amount of distance between your vibration and *Negative-Nelly's* vibration. The amount of distance between your vibration and someone else's vibration is equal to the amount of resistance (negativity) you feel when you are with them (or talk to them).

In the past you may have said "Hey, *Negative-Nelly* brings me down." The truth is *Negative-Nelly* didn't bring you down. You lowered your dial (vibration) to match theirs.

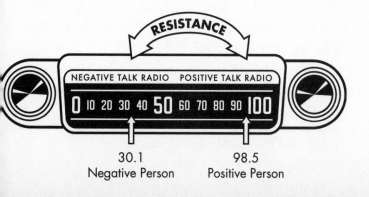

RESISTANCE

NEGATIVE TALK RADIO   POSITIVE TALK RADIO

0 10 20 30 40 **50** 60 70 80 90 **100**

30.1
Negative Person

98.5
Positive Person

How to HOLD Your Positive Vibration

What can you do in the future to maintain your vibration at 9? when you are talking to people who are at a much lower vibrat Just like you can select a station (or vibration) on your car radi you can also have a high vibration and stay there, despite havin *Negative-Nelly* in your life. Here's how to do that.

The next time your *Negative-Nelly* calls you and starts to talk al how sad their life is, or how they don't like their job, don't have enough money or a satisfying relationship, you have two choice

> **Choice #1:** You can buy into that conversation which
> then lowers your vibration to match theirs…
> or
> **Choice #2:** When you hear them say what they don't
> want, you can simply ask them "So, what do
> you want?"

Remember that as a *Negative-Nelly* goes from what they don't to what they do want, their words change, and when their wor change, their vibration changes so they now offer a new higher vibration. As their vibration rises it gets closer to matching you and the closer their vibration is to yours, the more harmonious your vibrations become.

Now you understand that when you meet somebody and you hit it off with them, saying to yourself "Did I ever click with them. Our chemistry was so good," you really mean that you vibrations are in harmony. When you meet somebody and be you even learn their name, you catch yourself saying "Wow, I don't like their energy. They're not my type," it's an indicator that your vibrations are not in harmony.

Your job is to look after your vibration and steer any conversat that you have with people to be more uplifting and positive. do that by remembering to gently ask the question "So, what do you want?," thus helping the other person achieve a more positive and therefore higher vibration.

tracting Your Ideal Relationship

I'll use the word 'relationship' here to indicate many kinds of relationships – perhaps your ideal partner, business relationship, your relationship with your children, parents, neighbors, work colleagues, students or clients.

Now we'll get started by using the 3-step formula for Law of Attraction to learn how to attract your ideal relationship.

> **Reminder:** The Contrast you've experienced in the past will be helpful for your future.

Knowing what you didn't like about a past partner or a past date is very useful to you. You can use this information to help you get clarity about the kind of partner you do want. For example, if you don't want someone who works too much, what do you want? If you don't want someone who is not adventurous, what do you want? If you don't want someone who is not interested in dancing, who is not romantic, or not a good listener etc., what do you want?

Understanding what you don't want will help you generate more clarity about what you do want and your clarity becomes your new, clear desire! The easiest way to do this is to say to yourself "So, what do I want?" It sounds simple and it is! When you change your observation from what you don't want to what you do want, the vibration changes. When you change your vibration, the results will change! Notice too, how you feel when you get clear about something. It feels good when we say "Oh! That's exactly what I'd like!" This new clarity has now become your desire and that is the first step to manifesting your ideal relationship.

If you're not truly offering a vibration of the way you want it be, then the Law of Attraction cannot respond to it. In other words, you are saying that you want THIS kind of person but you are sending out a vibe that is different than your desire. C way to check what vibration you are sending out is to observe what you ARE receiving in your life. It's always a perfect matc to whatever you are offering 'vibrationally'.

Most people while in the process of attracting their ideal relationship will often spend time noticing that they have NC been attracting exactly what they want. That noticing is causin them to send out the vibration of lack (a negative vibration). Stop observing what you are NOT attracting and you'll stop giving it your attention, energy and focus. Your job is to look for the parts of a relationship or the characteristics of a date tl ARE matching your desire list and give those your attention! Your vibration will change and the Law of Attraction will brir you more of the same!

Tip #1: Don't tell anyone your date was a flop!

Don't email your friends about it! Don't talk about it with your girlfriends! Don't write about it in your journal! Remember that the Law of Attraction doesn't know if you are remembering something, complaining about it, or worrying about it. The Law of Attraction will simply bring you more of whatever it is you are focusing on!

Tip #2: Build your Contrast list

Come home from your date and build a list of all the things that you didn't like about your dating experience and convert each item of contrast on your list into another thing that you clearly want.

Tip #3: Move on if it doesn't feel right

If it didn't feel good on the first date, it usually doesn't get better, so simply move on to the next date, adding to your Clarity list each time.

Tip #4: Tell why it matches

Spend time talking about it, writing about it, and daydreaming about what IS matching. Give what you like more attention, energy and focus.

Wrapping Up: Relationships and Your Vibration

Here's what we've covered in this section

◆ At every moment you are sending a vibration, either positive or negative

◆ When your vibration is high and someone else's is lower than yours, you feel resistance (negative vibration)

◆ To help maintain a high vibration when dealing with others who have a lower vibration ask them "So, what do you want?" when they are complaining or talking about what they don't want

◆ Use the Deliberate Attraction process to attract your ideal relationship

◆ **Four tips for attracting your ideal relationship:**

 – Don't tell anyone your date was a flop

 – Build a list

 – Move on if it doesn't feel right

 – Tell why it matches

arn How to Teach the
w of Attraction to Children

Imagine having everyone in your family or classroom practicing the Law of Attraction. This section is dedicated to giving you information, tools and fun games to help you teach the message of the Law of Attraction to children in an easy way.

When teaching adults, it is common to use words like 'manifestation', 'vibrations', 'synchronicity', 'serendipity' and 'coincidence'. When teaching the Law of Attraction to children, it is important to talk to them at their level using words they can relate to.

Tip #1: Keep your words simple!

Instead of using the word vibration, use *vibes*.

Recently, when asked to speak to a group of 10-year-olds in their classroom, I decided to begin my presentation by using a word they could relate to. My question to them was "Can you give me some examples of *negative vibes*?" I used the word *vibes* in place of *vibration*. The students quickly waved their hands in the air. These are some of the examples they shared:

- When my Mom doesn't have her coffee, she has negative vibes.
- When my parents fight in the house, I can feel negative vibes.
- When I see a bully at school, I feel negative vibes.
- Being in a scary building that's dark gives me negative vibes.

Clearly these kids knew exactly what a negative *vibe* was and they agreed that being around others who had negative vibes or having a negative vibe themselves was not a great feeling to have.

Tip #2: Get children to 'buy in' or 'own' a new concept by getting them to answer questions *from their own experience*.

Next I used a picture of a light switch on the blackboard, showing the 'on' and 'off' position. 'On' meant you had a positive vibe and 'Off' meant you had switched off your positive vibe and had a negative vibe instead. After having the students agree it felt better to have a positive vibe instead of negative one, I asked them if they wanted to learn how to change the negative vibe to a positive vibe. They all excitedly said "Yes."

I asked them to write these three words down in their notebooks in big letters: **DON'T, NOT** and **NO.** I then explained that when we use these words we feel negative. I asked them to give me examples of when these words were used in their lives. You can bet they had quite a list to give me. Here are some examples:

◆ Don't be late.
◆ Don't get your clothes dirty.
◆ Do not run in the halls.
◆ Don't leave your coats on the floor.
◆ No bullying.
◆ Don't play ball in the house.
◆ Don't eat or drink near the computer.

After making a list of all the examples on the blackboard, I suggested we read them together out loud. They all agreed that just saying the list out loud did indeed feel negative. In other words, I proved the point and they agreed. In doing so, I had surfaced the problem and next I presented them with a solution

Tip #3: Kids love a secret.

Choosing my words carefully once again, I told them I would teach them a 'secret' way to turn the light switch from the 'Off' (negative vibe) position to the 'On' (positive vibe) position. I intentionally chose the word 'secret' because I knew they would treat it as something special and really want to remember it. They loved it when I told them that this 'secret' was one that very few grown-ups knew, and that with this 'secret' they could change any negative vibe into a positive one.

The students learned that the secret to switching their vibes was to ask themselves a very simple question. Each time they heard themselves saying **don't, not** or **no,** they were to ask themselves "So, what do I want?" Revisiting their list of don't, not and no's, we came up with a "So, what do I want?" list. The students were eager to share their answers to this secret question.

Don't, Not and No	So, What Do I Want?
Don't be late	Arrive on time
Don't get your clothes dirty	Keep your clothes clean
Do not run in the halls	Walk in the halls
Don't leave your coats on the floor	Hang up your coats
No bullying	Play nicely
Don't play ball in the house	Play ball outside
Don't eat or drink at the computer	Eat or drink at the table

As I reviewed this list with the students, they all agreed that saying what they did want felt better than saying what they didn't want.

By applying Tips 1, 2 and 3, these students grasped the entire concept of changing their vibration from negative to positive – easily and quickly!

I knew they'd be going home eager and enthusiastic to share this message with their parents and friends. So again, I reminded them they had a secret, and in order to keep the secret special, they needed to be gentle when telling others about it. This way, the next time their parents, siblings or friends used the words **don't, not** and **no,** they could *gently* ask the secret question "So, what do you want?"

Positive
love, excitement,
joy, fun, safe

Negative
scared, angry, sad,
left-out, lonely

ols for Teaching the
w of Attraction to Children

Tool #1: Magnetic Board Game

An easy game to implement within any family or small group of children is the **Don't, Not and No Magnetic Board Game.** Prepare a magnetic board (or something similar) by writing the name of each family or group member across the top. Using fun magnets, the objective of the game is to get and keep the most magnets under your name at the end of each week. Start off by giving each person five magnets. Each time a member hears anyone using the words **don't, not** and **no,** the player who used those words loses a magnet to the player who noticed. Decide on a reward for the winner at the end of the week and keep it fun. Display your magnetic board in a central location. For families, an ideal place would be near your dinner table or on your fridge door so you can refer to it often. This is a fun game so parents and teachers – you play too!

Tool #2: On-Off Light Switch Poster

This poster will be a useful visual aid for younger children. Use it to help them understand the difference between feeling negative and positive emotions or vibes. I've included the following illustration to use as a guide.

First, together with the child, build a list of words that represent negative and positive emotions. Have the child help you place these words describing positive emotions on the 'ON' side of the light switch poster. Do the same for the words describing negative emotions, placing them on the 'OFF' side. As a parent or teacher, whenever you notice a child expressing an emotion, use the poster and have them find that emotion on the 'OFF' side or 'ON' side of the light switch poster. This poster will help reinforce their understanding between positive and negative vibes. Display the poster somewhere prominent where you can refer to it often.

Tool #3: The Secret Question Reminder

The purpose of this tool is to help children remember the secret question whenever they use the words **don't, not** and **no**. Using a wide rubber band, or a medallion, have your child or student label it "Secret." Now the child can wear it as a tool to help them remember to ask themselves "So, what do I want?"

Tool #4: Family or Group Meeting

For older children and teens, a weekly meeting can be a good way to learn and share about the Law of Attraction. I've included a list of questions that you can incorporate into your meetings.

◆ Are you noticing that you are reducing the number of times you use **don't, not** and **no**?

◆ When have you caught yourself using **don't, not** and **no**?

◆ Who have you taught or shared the Law of Attraction with this week?

◆ What evidence have you noticed that you are attracting more of what you want and less of what you don't?

◆ What would you like to attract more of this week?

To continue practicing the Law of Attraction between meetings, make sure everyone has each other's permission to give support in asking "So, what do you want?" Ask permission and give permission. *"Do I have your permission to mention when I notice you using* don't, not *and* no? *I give you my permission to point out to me every time you notice I'm using them!"*

Here's what we've covered in this section

- Simple words like *vibe* and *secret* are powerful teaching tools
- Ask questions that get kids to relate to concepts from their own experience (buy-in!)
- Use visual aids with younger children (light switch poster)
- Reinforce with games and rewards
- Parents – be sure to participate
- Ask permission and give permission
- Keep it fun

Putting It All Together

Now that you've learned how to use the Law of Attraction to get more of what you want, and less of what you don't want, you can start using the exercises and tools from this book right away.

Remember, the worksheets for Step 1, 2 and 3 plus bonus worksheets are available online for free.

Visit: www.LawofAttractionBook.com/worksheets.html

Refer to this book often for guidance. You can also make use of other resources such as articles, TeleClasses, seminars, my month e-zine, and my website: www.LawofAttractionBook.com

You now have the tools to let the Law of Attraction improve life. I wish you pure joy.

Michael

aying Connected to the Message of e Law of Attraction

pport and Resources

◆ Surrounding yourself with others who practice the Law of Attraction will help you to consistently offer a positive vibration, but how do you go about finding these people? One way is to use the Deliberate Attraction process. Use the power of the Law of Attraction to bring like-minded people into your life.

◆ Start a Law of Attraction group in your city. Find out more at www.lawofattractionbook.com/LOAdiscussiongroup.htm On this page you'll find information on how to host your own Law of Attraction discussion group.

◆ Read other books dedicated to the Law of Attraction. You'll find a list at: www.LawofAttractionBook.com/resources.html

References and Suggested Reading

Atkinson, William Walter (first edition 1906)
Thought Vibration or the Law of Attraction in the Thought Wor
Kessinger Publishing Company, 1998

Hanson, Rebecca *Law of Attraction for Business*
Rebecca Hanson Publisher, 2004

Hicks, Jerry and Esther *Ask and It Is Given, Learning to Man*
Your Desire (The Teachings of Abraham)
Hay House Inc., 2005

Hill, Napoleon (first edition 1937) *Think and Grow Rich*
Renaissance Books, 2001

Holliwell, Dr. Raymond *Working with the Law*
DeVorss & Company, 2005

Holmes, Ernest (1926) (revised edition 1938)
Basic Ideas of Science of Mind
DeVorss & Company, 1957

Murphy, Dr. Joseph *The Power of the Subconscious Mind*
Reward/Prentice Hall, 1963

Peale, Norman Vincent *The Power of Positive Thinking*
Ballantine Books, 1952

Ponder, Catherine *Dynamic Law of Prosperity*
DeVorss & Company, 1985

Tracy, Brian *Universal Law of Success and Achievement*
Nightingale-Conant Corporation, 1991

Wattles, Wallace *The Science of Getting Rich*
Top of the Mountain Publishing, 1910

ecial Appreciation

was highly motivated and inspired by the works of Esther and Jerry Hicks of Abraham-Hicks Publications. It is with deep appreciation that I thank them for sharing their knowledge of the Law of Attraction with the world and with me. My life is fuller and richer because of it.

For more information about Abraham-Hicks Publications visit: www.abraham-hicks.com or call 830-755-2299.

I owe a heartfelt and much deserved thank-you to the tens of thousands of people who have attended all of my seminars and TeleClasses; the multitude of e-mails I've received telling me of your personal success stories; the hundreds of people who have called in to speak to me during my many radio talk show broadcasts – YOU are what makes MY Law of Attraction work!

Also, to all of the people who have been there with me since the beginning, supporting me physically, emotionally and spiritually – my love to you always.

In this powerful book, Michael J. Losier shows
you how you can build strong relationships—
at home or in the workplace.

Please turn this page for
a preview of

Law of Connection

Available in hardcover

PART I

THE 3 CONDITIONS FOR CONNECTING

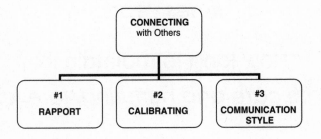

RAPPORT

How long to build it?

*Sometimes seconds and some-
times years.*

How long to maintain it?

With care and nurturing, forever

How long to break it?

Only seconds.

How long to repair it?

Sometimes never.

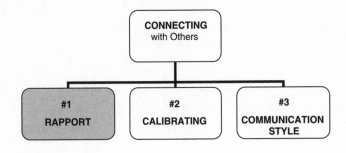

Many of us can recall a time when we have met someone we instantly liked—or someone we instantly disliked, despite having something in common with that person.

> **rap·port**, noun
> relationship; esp., a close or sympathetic relationship; agreement; harmony

Building rapport with a person can happen instantly or it can take a while to develop.

Rapport is a key part of communication. Communication happens on two levels—verbal and nonverbal.

There are two common ways most people either fail to achieve or break rapport with others: by not picking up on verbal and nonverbal cues to the other person's communication style, and through miscommunication, because one person doesn't understand the other's style. *Law of Connection* will give you all the tools you need to achieve, and not break, rapport.

Calibrating—Condition 2

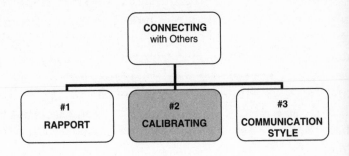

Calibrating is the art of paying attention and respondir
to what you've noticed. It's about picking up on the ve
and nonverbal cues (such as laughing, blushing, nail-bi
or stammering) that indicate another person's mental o
emotional state and then adjusting your own commun
tion style to match or accommodate theirs. By calibrati
you build rapport.

When you don't pay attention, you could end up maki
assumptions or jumping to conclusions without really
knowing what the other person is thinking or feeling.
When you fail to calibrate your style to theirs, you cou
end up breaking rapport.

People who are good calibrators are able to quickly asse
situation and respond to it in a way that establishes an
maintains rapport. As a result, other people find it easy
have them around. Not being able to calibrate is anno
and frustrating to others and causes misunderstanding
break rapport.

Here are three examples of how calibrating works.

ming home from work:

A working couple arrives home within thirty minutes of each other. The husband arrives first. When the wife gets home she is bursting with excitement about having received a huge promotion. However, she notices immediately that her husband is still wearing his jacket and tie and is slamming and banging things around in the kitchen. Based on those two cues, she knows that something is wrong. Instead of sharing her good news immediately, she creates rapport by going into the kitchen to greet him, express her concern, and ask how he's doing.

ving diners in a restaurant:

Two friends having dinner together are in the middle of a serious conversation when their overly cheerful server bounds up and, without paying any attention to the mood at the table, announces with a big smile, "Hi there, I'm Biff, I'll be your server tonight!" The server hasn't noticed the seriousness of the diners' mood and has failed to calibrate his style to theirs—thereby sabotaging himself by failing to build the rapport he had intended to create.

ering a library vs. a cafeteria:

As a loud group of teenagers leaves the noisy cafeteria and enters the library, they immediately calibrate and adjust the volume of their conversation to match the quiet of the library. This establishes rapport with everyone who is already working quietly in the room.

y often you have only nonverbal cues to help you brate another person's mental or emotional state. Here a number of nonverbal cues you can watch out for to p increase your calibrating skills.

Examples of Nonverbal Cues That Indicate Mood

Blushing	Turning pale	Blue lips
Gasping for air	Rapid breathing	Shallow breathing
Giggling	Pacing the floor	Sweating
Laughing	Wringing hands	Biting fingernails
Whispering	Upright posture	Slouched over
Stammering	Staying silent	Repeatedly checking ti
Smiling	Frowning	Wiggling

You will no doubt have many opportunities to observe
verbal cues at work, in your primary relationship, and w
your entire family. Now that you are aware of these cue
you will certainly notice when others have not calibrate
well. You will come to see and understand the direct lin
between calibrating well and increasing rapport—as wel
how failing to calibrate breaks the connection.

derstanding Communication
les—Condition 3

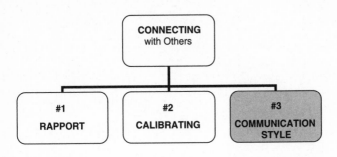

he third condition for creating connection, understanding thers' communication styles, is so important that I have evoted fully one-third of this book to teaching you how to o it.

our ability to understand and match another person's ommunication style is what will make you a good calibra- or and keep you in rapport so that there is a good connec- on between you. Not understanding someone else's style quite often the reason two people are not connecting.

he four communication styles are Visual, Auditory, Kines- hetic, and Digital.

Vhether you are communicating with a group or an individ- al, understanding each of the four communication styles rill help you stay in rapport and connection.

n Part III I'll be helping you to learn and understand more bout each of these styles, but first I'm going to ask you to omplete the ten-question self-assessment on the following ages. Don't overthink it; just answer the questions quickly nd intuitively.

out the Author

Michael Losier writes and teaches about a subject he knows very well. Over the years, Michael Losier has done a complete overhaul of his life. Although he is quick to point out that he's always had a happy life, including an untroubled childhood and a supportive family, Michael clearly states that his discovery and application of the Law of Attraction is responsible for the new level of success and fulfillment he enjoys as an author, trainer and entrepreneur.

Michael Losier grew up in a blue-collar community in New Brunswick, Canada. A student of NLP (Neuro-Linguistic Programming, a technology of psychological and behavioral modification), Losier and four other NLP students in Victoria, BC produced a successful series of annual holistic health expos beginning in 1990. In the mid-90s, Losier participated in programs that trained him as an "Empowerment Coach," and in 1995 he became a certified NLP practitioner. He then shortened his work week with the government to four days, and spent his fifth weekday coaching clients.

In 1995, Losier was introduced to the subject of Law of Attraction. This led him to wonder why he ever attracted anything negative to his life. Michael then explored Huna (the Hawaiian metaphysical system), Feng Shui and other energy-based subjects. He concluded that any topic needed to be taught in a model that people could easily embrace. "It had to be made user-friendly," he recalls.

In 1996, Michael began weekly meetings with one other Law of Attraction enthusiast. This quickly grew to a roster of 45 people meeting every two weeks. He then created Teleclass International Inc., with a business partner. TeleClasses are live, interactive training classes conducted over the telephone using state-of-the-art teleconferencing bridge systems. Losier has reached over 15,000 people a year via TeleClasses.

Michael Losier is a passionate, committed man. He is a faculty member of the Law of Attraction Training Center which trains students to become Law of Attraction Certified Practitioners.

Michael logs hundreds of hours a year as a radio and TV talk-show guest and is also a frequent keynote speaker/trainer at Positive Living Centers, spiritual centers, businesses, corporatie and conventions in the U.S., Canada and Mexico.

When Michael gets his way – and he often does when it come to spreading the message of Law of Attraction – millions will soon be using his powerful system to improve their lives. This will be a true win-win outcome for all concerned.

When Michael isn't teaching, leading or learning, he enjoys hiking through old-growth forests of the Pacific Northwest an tending to his patio garden in Victoria, B.C., Canada.

Introduction

Nothing is more exciting than WWE! Whether you're watching all the action on *Monday Night Raw*, checking out the powerslams on *Friday Night SmackDown*, finding new foes on *WWE Superstars*, meeting the new generation of Superstars on *WWE NXT*, or seeing new champions crowned at the big pay-per-view events, WWE is always a blast to watch.

This book is your guide to the WWE Universe. Here you'll learn everything there is to know about sports entertainment. You'll become an expert on all things WWE! From the Superstars to the Divas to the pay-per-view events, this book has it all! So get ready to enter the ring!

Contents

RAW

Where It All Started:
History of *Monday Night Raw*

When *Monday Night Raw* aired for the first time on January 11, 1993, everything changed for WWE. Held in a large ballroom in the Manhattan Center in New York City, the first episode of *Raw* was broadcast live across the world. Since then, it has become one of the longest-running weekly episodic (meaning there is a new episode every week) television series in TV history.

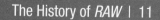

During the 1990s, *Raw* competed against its rival company, World Championship Wrestling (WCW), but it quickly became known as the more extreme of the two shows. That's because *Raw* brought about the rise of "Stone Cold" Steve Austin, The Rock, D-Generation X, Chris Jericho, Edge, and many more. By 2001, *Raw* was victorious in its war with WCW. Mr. McMahon, who was in charge of the WWE, bought WCW, but the future for WCW and its Superstars was unknown. No one knew if the WCW Superstars would continue to work in sports entertainment. But Mr. McMahon was smart and realized that they could *all* work for him! Lots of WCW Superstars were hired by WWE, which created a huge group of performers to choose from in the company.

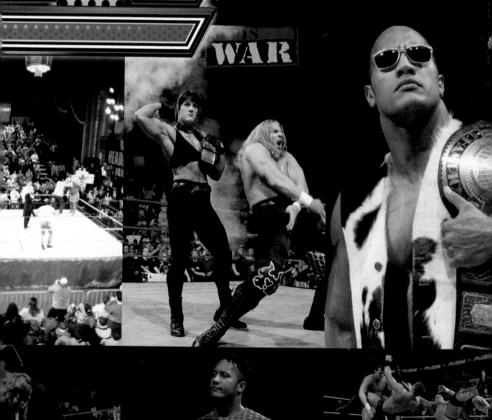

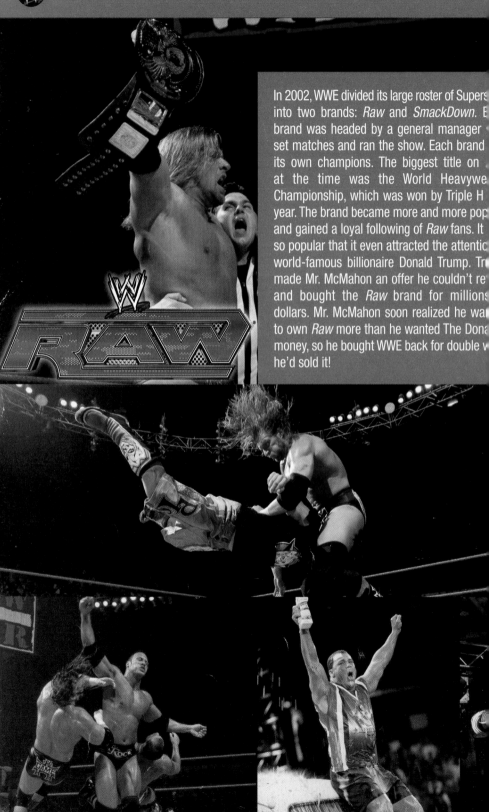

In 2002, WWE divided its large roster of Supers
into two brands: *Raw* and *SmackDown*. E
brand was headed by a general manager
set matches and ran the show. Each brand
its own champions. The biggest title on
at the time was the World Heavywe
Championship, which was won by Triple H
year. The brand became more and more pop
and gained a loyal following of *Raw* fans. It
so popular that it even attracted the attentic
world-famous billionaire Donald Trump. Tr
made Mr. McMahon an offer he couldn't re
and bought the *Raw* brand for millions
dollars. Mr. McMahon soon realized he wa
to own *Raw* more than he wanted The Dona
money, so he bought WWE back for double v
he'd sold it!

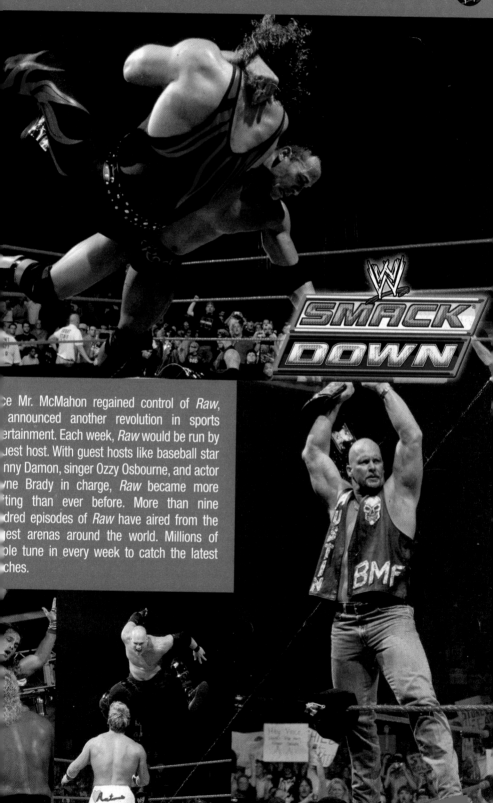

ce Mr. McMahon regained control of *Raw*,
announced another revolution in sports
ertainment. Each week, *Raw* would be run by
uest host. With guest hosts like baseball star
nny Damon, singer Ozzy Osbourne, and actor
ne Brady in charge, *Raw* became more
ting than ever before. More than nine
dred episodes of *Raw* have aired from the
est arenas around the world. Millions of
ple tune in every week to catch the latest
ches.

Ever since *Raw* premiered in 1993, it has featured the hottest Superstars and Divas in WW. All-time greats like Bret "Hit Man" Hart, Shawn Michaels, Undertaker, "Stone Cold" Steve Aust and The Rock ignited the *Raw* flame and passed it on to Superstars like Triple H, John Cena, a Randy Orton. Today, a rising generation of Superstars such as Sheamus, The Miz, Evan Bourr and Ted DiBiase are fighting their ways to the top of WWE.

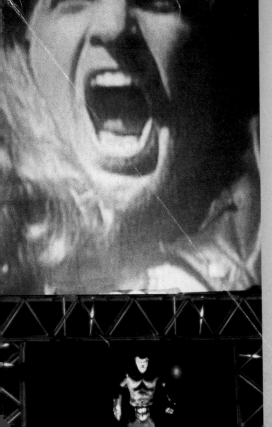

don't forget about the *Raw* Divas! They are definitely tough. No
tter if you tune in to see the Superstars, the Divas, or both, it's no
der *Raw* has lasted so long. Nothing in sports or entertainment
more talented people, more exciting action, or better stories
Monday Night Raw.

JOHN CENA

HEIGHT: 6 feet 1 inch
WEIGHT: 240 pounds
FROM: West Newbury, Massachusetts
WWE DEBUT: 2002

SIGNATURE MOVES:
Attitude Adjustment, STF

ACCOMPLISHMENTS:
World Heavyweight Champion, WWE Champion, United States Champion, World Tag Team Champion, Royal Rumble Winner (2008)

JOHN·CEN

Since joining WWE in 2002, John Cena has used his talents and charming personality to win over WWE fans. Cena has to great heights, capturing both the WWE Championsh and the World Heavyweight Championship. Known for his rivalries with Superstars such as Randy Orton, Edge, and Sheamus, Cena has defeated everyone he's battled.

John Cena is an explosive competitor. He loves his fans and is committed to giving them a great match each and every time he steps into the ring! He even volunteers in his free time, which makes him a role model for kids everywhere. Cena is honest, never cheats in his matches, and loves his fans. Even though he's already a huge star in the ring, Cena wanted to become a name in Hollywood, too. He starred in action movies like *The Marine* and *12 Rounds* and showed his softer side on the Nickelodeon series *True Jackson, VP.* Even though he enjoyed his time making movies, Cena has repeatedly said that he will never lea WWE or sports entertainment. He loves the WW Universe—and his fans—too much to ever do that.

CENA APPROVED

TRIPLE H

HEIGHT: 6 feet 4 inches
WEIGHT: 255 pounds
FROM: Greenwich, Connecticut
WWE DEBUT: 1995

SIGNATURE MOVE: Pedigree

ACCOMPLISHMENTS:
WWE Champion, World Heavyweight Champion, Intercontinental Champion, Unified WWE Tag Team Champion, World Tag Team Champion, European Champion, King of the Ring (1997), Royal Rumble Winner (2002)

triple h

For nearly two decades, Triple H has won championshi championship, and defeated just about every WWE Sup that he's ever faced. With his trusty sledgehammer side, Triple H always has a plan. He's so smart that he e the nickname "The Cerebral Assassin." Whether as the of D-Generation X or as a solo competitor, Triple H is a unstoppable.

He calls himself "The Game" and "The King of because no one can defeat him. With an arsenal of that he learned through a lifetime of studying master as Harley Race, Jack Brisco, and Dusty Rhodes, Triple for this business. He is perhaps the most drive determined of all WWE Superstars. He wants to be th Champion forever, and he won't let anything stand in h until that is a reality. Millions of members of the WWE U chant his name and cheer in excitement when he arenas around the world. It's time to play the game!

RANDY ORTON

HEIGHT: 6 feet 4 inches
WEIGHT: 245 pounds
FROM: St. Louis, Missouri
WWE DEBUT: 2002

SIGNATURE MOVE: RKO

ACCOMPLISHMENTS:
WWE Champion, World
Heavyweight Champion,
Intercontinental Champion,
World Tag Team Champion,
Royal Rumble Winner (2009)

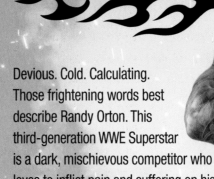

Devious. Cold. Calculating. Those frightening words best describe Randy Orton. This third-generation WWE Superstar is a dark, mischievous competitor who loves to inflict pain and suffering on his opponents. Known as "The Viper," Orton strikes quickly and powerfully. Orton earned his tough reputation by becoming the youngest World Heavyweight Championship winner in history. He battled Triple H throughout the years, and he even once attacked Triple H's wife, Stephanie McMahon! Of course, that made Triple H and the entire McMahon family hate Orton.

Orton led a group of young second- and third-generation Superstars known as Legacy. But he eventually got rid of his followers and started down the path of good. Don't let his new, more heroic attitude fool you—he will attack anyone who opposes him and, like a viper, will bite his prey when they least expect it.

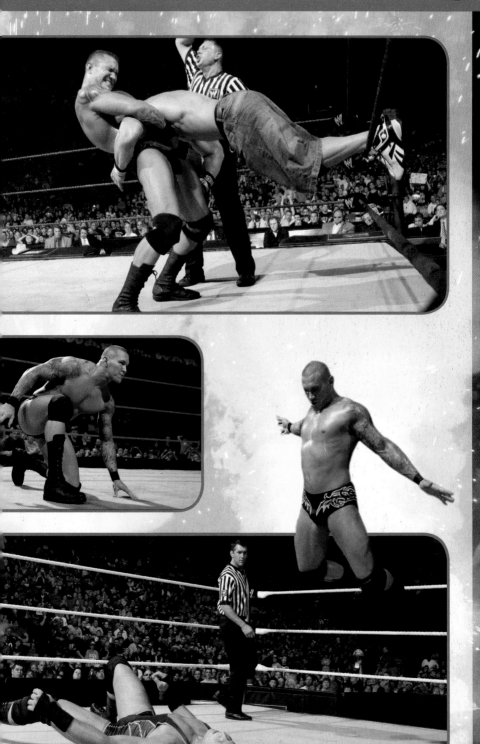

CM PUNK

HEIGHT: 6 feet 1 inch
WEIGHT: 222 pounds
FROM: Chicago, Illinois
WWE DEBUT: 2006

SIGNATURE MOVES:
G.T.S. (Go to Sleep),
Anaconda Vise

ACCOMPLISHMENTS:
World Heavyweight
Champion, ECW Champion,
World Tag Team Champion,
Intercontinental Champion

CM Punk is known as the "Straight Edge Superstar," wh
means that he doesn't involve himself in anything that
could potentially harm his body (other than
wrestling, that is!). CM Punk's other nickname
is the "Straight Edge Savior," which he earned
by making it his personal mission to "save" the
WWE Superstars, Divas, and the entire WWE
Universe from evil habits.

When he's not on a mission to save the world,
Punk likes to kick butt in the ring. He's even
won a World Heavyweight Championship!
No wonder he has so many loyal followers,
such as the former members of the Straight
Edge Society and, currently, The New Nexus.
Though Punk still takes every opportunity he can to
people about his beliefs, even if he's in the middle
match! But that doesn't mean he isn't a serious conter
Thanks to his patented Go to Sleep kick and Anaconda
sleeperhold, CM Punk has had his fair share of victories

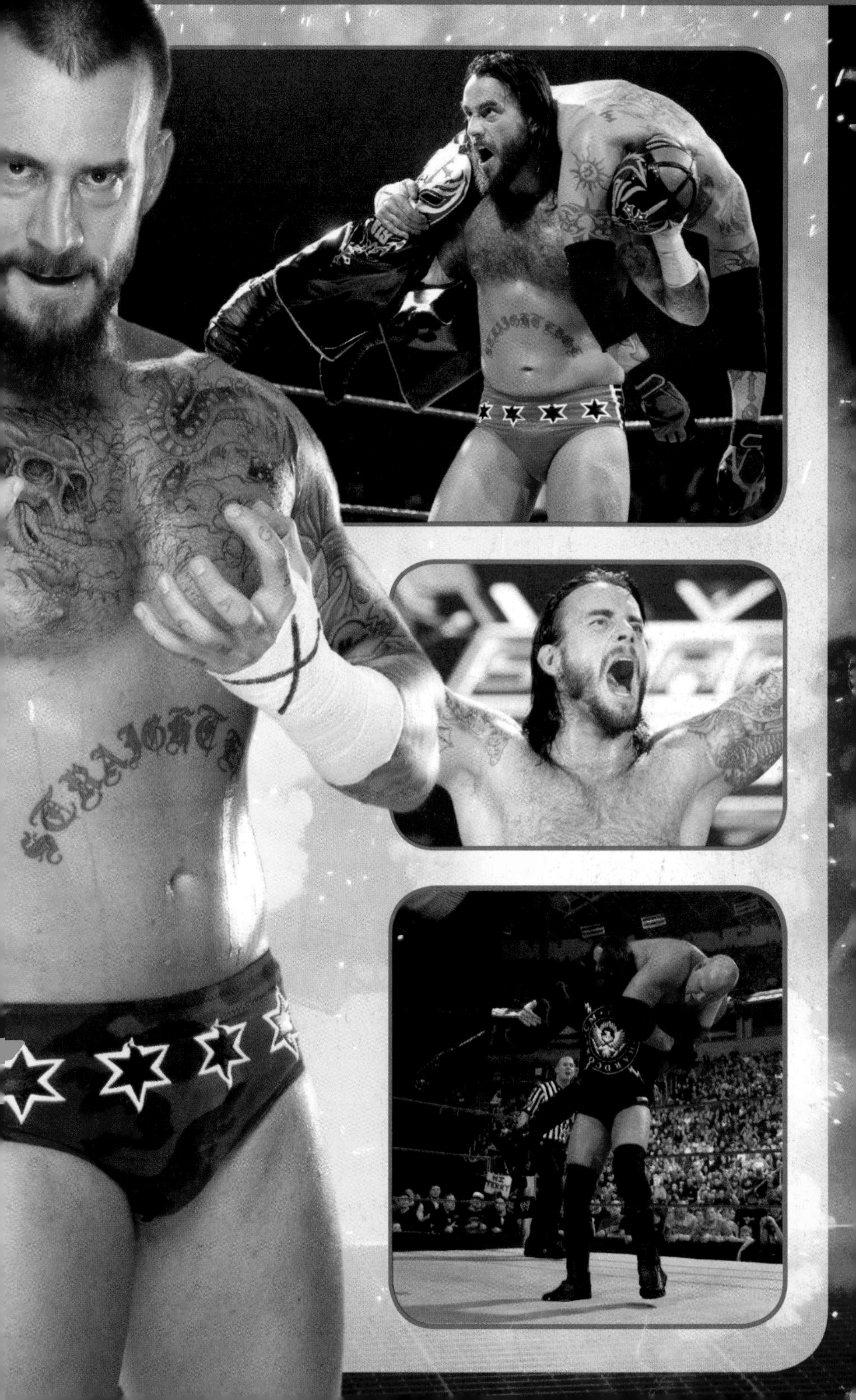

CHRIS JERICHO

HEIGHT: 6 feet
WEIGHT: 226 pounds
FROM: Winnipeg, Manitoba
WWE DEBUT: 1999

SIGNATURE MOVES:
The Codebreaker,
the Walls of Jericho

ACCOMPLISHMENTS:
WWE Champion, World
Heavyweight Champion,
WCW Champion,
Intercontinental Champion,
European Champion,
Hardcore Champion, Unified
Tag Team Champion, ECW TV
Champion, WCW TV Champion,
WCW Cruiserweight Champion

Chris Jericho burst onto the WWE scene by interru[
speech by The Rock on *Monday Night Raw*. Talk ab
entrance! Chris Jericho first got into sports entertainm
competing in matches in Mexico and Japan. He was
trained to wrestle by the Hart family, the most famous
wrestling family in Canada. Jericho has beaten the
best in the business. He was the first to hold the
WWE Championship and the WCW Championship
simultaneously, defeating both The Rock and
"Stone Cold" Steve Austin in the same night.

Jericho spends his time out of the ring as a
rock star. No, really—he is the lead singer of
a heavy metal band called Fozzy! Once
beloved by the WWE Universe, Jericho has
turned his back on the fans because he feels
they are all liars and don't deserve his love. He has wor
more championships, been in the main event of more
live events, and defeated more talented performers
than almost any other WWE Superstar. And if you
don't believe it, just ask him. He doesn't mind telling y[

SHEAMUS

HEIGHT: 6 feet 6 inches
WEIGHT: 272 pounds
FROM: Dublin, Ireland
WWE DEBUT: 2009

SIGNATURE MOVE: Crucifix Bomb

ACCOMPLISHMENTS:
WWE Champion, WWE King of the Ring (2010)

haps no other WWE Superstar has had a faster rise to stardom than the "Celtic Warrior" eamus. After a short stint in Extreme Championship Wrestling, Sheamus joined *Raw* became a two-time WWE champion—the first in his rookie year! Sheamus is a tough nman who can boast victories over John Cena, Triple H, and Randy Orton. With such a ong beginning to his WWE career, Sheamus's star will only continue to shine brighter.

THE MIZ ™

The Miz is awesome, and he won't mind telling you so. This former reality TV star is a fierce competitor. He wants to win at everything he does and will tear down any obstacle. It doesn't matter if it's in popular TV shows, like *Real World* and *Fear Factor*, or the WWE ring. The Miz is determined to showcase his awesomeness no matter the cost. And he's won the titles to prove it.

I'M AWESOME

THE MIZ

HEIGHT: 6 feet 1 inch
WEIGHT: 231 pounds
FROM: Cleveland, Ohio
WWE DEBUT: 2006

SIGNATURE MOVE:
Skull-Crushing Finale

ACCOMPLISHMENTS:
United States Champion,
Unified Tag Team Champion,
WWE Champion

DANIEL BRYAN

HEIGHT: 5 feet 10 inches
WEIGHT: 190 pounds
FROM: Aberdeen, Washington
WWE DEBUT: 2010

ACCOMPLISHMENT:
United States Champion

DANIEL BRYAN

Daniel Bryan has competed in sports entertainment for almost ten years. He made a name for himself in independent matches around the world, which earned him a loyal fan base. He has perfected his in-ring skills and become a solid and talented competitor. He knows lots of moves and counter-moves and can beat almost any opponent he wrestles. But he knew he could go only so far in his career wrestling in independent matches. Daniel made the move to WWE and worked hard to prove himself in the ring. It all paid off when he took home his first title: the United States Championship.

THE HART DYNASTY

Third-generation Superstar Da
Hart Smith has a tremendo
legacy to live up to. The grands
of WWE Hall of Famer Stu H
and son of the late "Briti
Bulldog" Davey Boy Smi
David is a powerhouse in t
ring. With his knowledge
classic submission holds and I
strength and agility, David h
proven to be a formidable oppone
He's got the genes and training to be one of the WW
most legendary Superstars someday—just like his o
and grandfather were before him.

DAVID HART SMITH

HEIGHT: 6 feet 5 inches
WEIGHT: 250 pounds
FROM: Calgary, Alberta
WWE DEBUT: 2009

SIGNATURE MOVE:
Running Powerslam

ACCOMPLISHMENT:
World Tag Team Champion

NATALYA

atalya holds some impressive "firsts" in her personal book of accomplishments. She was he first ever third-generation iva in the WWE—the randdaughter of WWE Hall f Famer Stu Hart and the aughter of former World Tag eam Champion Jim "The Anvil" eidhart. And she was the first art family member to hold the WE Divas Championship. With nazing technical skills in the ring at live up to her family's heritage, atalya has already shown that she is one the most dominant divas to ever compete the WWE.

NATALYA

HEIGHT: 5 feet 5 inches
FROM: Calgary, Alberta
WWE DEBUT: 2008

ACCOMPLISHMENT:
WWE Divas Champion

Natalya

Brash, arrogant, and extremely talented, Tyson Kidd burst onto the WWE scene as a member of the Hart Dynasty. But after breaking from his longtime friend and partner David Hart Smith, Kidd went on to find success and glory as a single Superstar. Kidd was trained by WWE Hall of Famer Stu Hart and boasts that he is the last graduate of Hart's infamous Hart Dungeon. With that level of training and talent, nothing can stop Tyson Kidd from accomplishing his dreams in the WWE.

TYSON KIDD

HEIGHT: 5 feet 9 inches
WEIGHT: 195 pounds
FROM: Calgary, Alberta
WWE DEBUT: 2009

SIGNATURE MOVE:
Sharpshooter

ACCOMPLISHMENT:
World Tag Team Champion

alicia FOX™

en WWE Superstar Edge and *SmackDown* eral manager Vickie Guerrero decided to married, they hired Alicia Fox as their lding planner. But Vickie thought Alicia s too pretty and threatened to fire her. e liked Alicia, though, and introduced her to WWE Universe. Alicia quickly fell in love the world of sports entertainment. gave up her career helping es pick their perfect wedding sses to become a WWE Diva. high-flying style brought Alicia he top of the Diva mountain in 0, when she captured the WWE s Championship.

ALICIA FOX

HEIGHT: 5 feet 9 inches
FROM: Tampa, Florida
WWE DEBUT: 2009

ACCOMPLISHMENT:
WWE Divas Champion

TED DiBIASE

As a third-generation WWE Superstar, Ted DiBiase had a lot of expectations to live up to. The son of WWE Hall of Famer the "Million Dollar Man" Ted DiBiase Sr., Ted quickly proved his strength as a member of Randy Orton's Legacy team. But Ted wanted to be more than just Orton's sidekick. He broke apart from Legacy and proved that he is indeed "priceless." He even conquered Hollywood as the star of *The Marine 2*.

TED DiBIASE

HEIGHT: 6 feet 3 inches
WEIGHT: 235 pounds
FROM: West Palm Beach, Florida
WWE DEBUT: 2008

SIGNATURE MOVE:
Dream Street

ACCOMPLISHMENT:
World Tag Team Champion

The Great KHALI ™

Maybe you wouldn't expect a monster like the Great Khali to be a flirt with the ladies of the WWE Universe, but that's exactly what he is! With the help of his trusty translator, Ranjin Singh, the former World Heavyweight Champion is the host of the Khali Kiss Cam. Khali actually handpicks a woman from the audience to kiss on-screen! While he may be known for his flirting, he is also a powerful WWE Superstar *and* a Hollywood movie star. He appeared in several big blockbusters including *The Longest Yard* and *Get Smart*.

GREAT KHALI

HEIGHT: 7 feet 3 inches
WEIGHT: 420 pounds
FROM: India
WWE DEBUT: 2006

ACCOMPLISHMENT:
World Heavyweight Champion

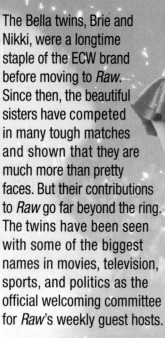

The Bella twins, Brie and Nikki, were a longtime staple of the ECW brand before moving to *Raw*. Since then, the beautiful sisters have competed in many tough matches and shown that they are much more than pretty faces. But their contributions to *Raw* go far beyond the ring. The twins have been seen with some of the biggest names in movies, television, sports, and politics as the official welcoming committee for *Raw*'s weekly guest hosts.

BELLA TWINS

BRIE • **HEIGHT:** 5 feet 6 inches

NIKKI • **HEIGHT:** 5 feet 6 inches

FROM: Scottsdale, Arizona
WWE DEBUT: 2008

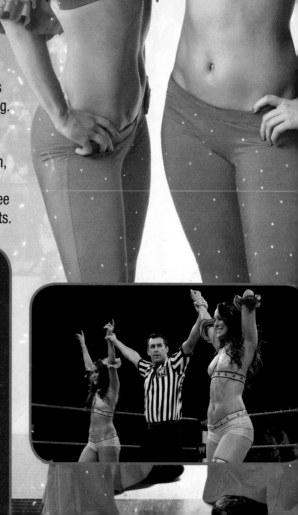

Primo

Growing up in San Juan, Puerto Rico, Primo longed to be a WWE Superstar. The son of a sports entertainment legend, Carlos Colon, Primo began training when he was only seven years old! By the time he was seventeen, Primo had proven he could dominate the sport he loved. A short time later, Primo joined WWE and teamed up with his brother, Carlito. The brothers were an unstoppable force and even won the first-ever Unified Tag Team Championship before going their separate ways.

PRIMO

HEIGHT: 5 feet 10 inches
WEIGHT: 218 pounds
FROM: San Juan, Puerto Rico
WWE DEBUT: 2008

SIGNATURE MOVE: Diving Headbutt

ACCOMPLISHMENT:
Unified Tag Team Champion

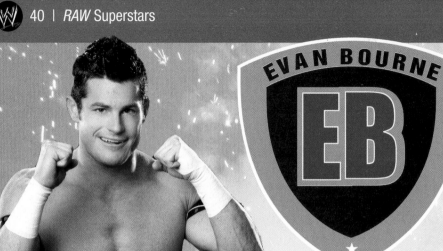

EVAN BOURNE

EB

Evan Bourne exploded onto the WWE scene in 2008. With an arsenal of aerial moves, Bourne is always fun to watch in the ring. As a lifelong sports entertainment fan, Evan Bourne was inspired by WWE legends such as Jimmy "Superfly" Snuka and "Flyin'" Brian Pillman. Much like his heroes, Evan Bourne hopes to soar to even greater heights in WWE by winning a championship.

EVAN BOURNE

HEIGHT: 5 feet 9 inches
WEIGHT: 183 pounds
FROM: St. Louis, Missouri
WWE DEBUT: 2008

SIGNATURE MOVE:
Shooting Star Press

A powerful mix of beauty and brains, Eve has become a Diva to watch as she rises through the ranks of WWE. Since winning the 2007 WWE Diva Search, Eve has chased after the WWE Women's and Divas Championships. As a former dancer for the L.A. Clippers, she was prepared for the competition and physical demands of WWE. She even won the Divas Championship in 2010!

EVE TORRES

HEIGHT: 5 feet 8 inches
FROM: Los Angeles, California
WWE DEBUT: 2007

ACCOMPLISHMENTS:
Divas Champion, WWE Diva Search Winner (2007)

WWE Diva Search: Every summer, talented women from across the country compete in the WWE Diva Search, hoping to win enough votes from fans to become the newest WWE Diva. The women give interviews, compete in physical challenges, and even enter the wrestling ring to show off their skills.

MARK HENRY ™

For more than a decade the "World's Strongest Man" Mark Henry has used his record-setting strength to become a major star in WWE. A former Olympic athlete in powerlifting, Henry has fought his way to victories on both *Raw* and *SmackDown*. A lot of WWE Superstars claim to be the biggest or the best, but Mark Henry is one of the few who can back up this claim—he set records in weight lifting in 1990 when he was only nineteen years old! It almost impossible for anyone to match his size and strength, which is what makes him an intimidating opponent.

MARK HENRY

HEIGHT: 6 feet 1 inch
WEIGHT: 392 pounds
FROM: Silsbee, Texas
WWE DEBUT: 1996

SIGNATURE MOVE:
World's Strongest Slam

ACCOMPLISHMENTS:
ECW Champion, United States Champion, European Champion

Gail Kim

Gail Kim burst onto the WWE scene by winning the Women's ampionship in her very first match! Gail came known for punishing other Divas in e ring with her tough moves. After king a few years off from WWE, Gail urned to *SmackDown* and then moved *Raw*, where she faced off with the men's and Divas Champions. Gail is a quest to regain the gold she once d, and it seems like no woman will and in her way!

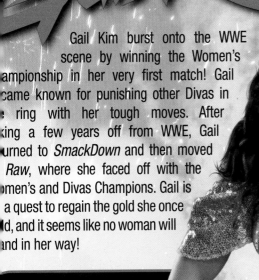

GAIL KIM

HEIGHT: 5 feet 4 inches
FROM: Toronto, Ontario
WWE DEBUT: 2002

ACCOMPLISHMENT:
Women's Champion

Goldust

Goldust is definitely the strangest Superstar ever to compete in WWE. His wacky costumes and face paint have been freaking out fans for more than a decade! Goldust uses the confusion and discomfort he creates with his costumes to psych out his opponents. He's won several titles and even battled WWE Hall of Famer "Rowdy" Roddy Piper in a Hollywood Backlot Brawl at WrestleMania. Being the oldest son of WWE Hall of Famer Dusty Rhodes only makes Goldust more unforgettable.

GOLDUST

HEIGHT: 6 feet 6 inches
WEIGHT: 260 pounds
FROM: Hollywood, California
WWE DEBUT: 1995

SIGNATURE MOVES:
Curtain Call, Golden Globes

ACCOMPLISHMENTS:
Intercontinental Champion,
World Tag Team Champion,
Hardcore Champion

John Morrison

ohn Morrison might be known for strutting own the red carpet at Hollywood events, but he's lso a solid competitor in the ring. Morrison's tough loves made him a multi-time tag team champion, ut he's just as strong a competitor when he's in le ring by himself. As a single, Morrison won the tercontinental Champion title. As long as lorrison doesn't focus too much on his looks and nage, he has a long career ahead of him in the ring.

JOHN MORRISON

HEIGHT: 6 feet 1 inch
WEIGHT: 223 pounds
FROM: Los Angeles, California
WWE DEBUT: 2005

SIGNATURE MOVES: Starship Pain, the Moonlight Drive

ACCOMPLISHMENTS: Intercontinental Champion, ECW Champion, WWE Tag Team Champion

Maryse

The French-Canadian powerhouse Maryse is a deceptive Diva. She'll say nice things to her opponents' faces in English and then turn around and say something rude in French! Maryse is arrogant and firmly believes she's better at everything than everyone else. When WWE Superstar The Miz tried to ask her out on a date, she shot him down! Despite her nasty attitude, Maryse is a talented performer in the ring. She's already won the Divas Championship and is convinced she's going to win it again. After all, there is no one more talented or better looking in WWE—at least, according to Maryse!

MARYSE

HEIGHT: 5 feet 8 inches
FROM: Montreal, Quebec
WWE DEBUT: 2006

ACCOMPLISHMENT:
Divas Champion

MELINA

...ywood photographers love Melina, and lucky for ...n, she loves having her picture taken! When ...'s not posing for the paparazzi, Melina is a tough ...petitor in the ring. At one time, she managed ...former boyfriend John Morrison. But after ...ding him to the Intercontinental Championship, ...ina decided to focus on her own goals. She ...ght her way to the top of the Diva division, capturing ...h the Women's Championship and the Divas ...mpionship along the way. Battling back from ...er-threatening injuries that forced her to undergo ...or knee surgery, Melina has proven time and time ...in that she is a force to be reckoned with.

MELINA

HEIGHT: 5 feet 4 inches
FROM: Los Angeles, California
WWE DEBUT: 2005

ACCOMPLISHMENTS:
Women's Champion,
Divas Champion

Most Dominant Diva & Sexiest Woman on T.V.

Santino

Santino Marella's WWE debut must have been the greatest night of his life. Santino came to a WWE match in Italy as a fan and left as a winner in the ring! Santino accepted an open challenge from then-Intercontinental Champion Umaga. Even though he was much smaller than his challenger, Santino defeated Umaga and captured the gold. Since then, the young Italian has entertained the WWE Universe with his goofy quirks, like purposely mispronouncing the names of the WWE Superstars. After winning his second Intercontinental Champion title, Santino set out on a mission to become the longest reigning champion, but fell short.

SANTINO MARELLA

HEIGHT: 5 feet 10 inches
WEIGHT: 227 pounds
FROM: Calabria, Italy
WWE DEBUT: 2007

SIGNATURE MOVE: The Cobra

ACCOMPLISHMENTS:
Intercontinental Champion, WWE
Tag Team Champion

R-Truth

What's up? What's up? WWE fans everywhere know -Truth by the familiar sound of his entrance. R-Truth definitely one of WWE's most exciting Superstars watch. But his talents go far beyond the ng. When he's not bodyslamming his oponents, R-Truth is an accomplished pper! R-Truth loves telling his fans at WWE helped get his life on track, d he encourages them to go after eir own dreams, too. Whether he's the ring or behind the mic, -Truth is always focused on s next big goal.

R-TRUTH

HEIGHT: 6 feet 2 inches
WEIGHT: 228 pounds
FROM: Charlotte, North Carolina
WWE DEBUT: 2000

SIGNATURE MOVE: Lie Detector

ACCOMPLISHMENT:
United States Champion

YOSHI TATSU

Tatsu shocked the WWE Universe when, in his debut match, he defeated Shelton Benjamin with a single kick! Tatsu's lightning-quick feet became the talk of the WWE. None of the Superstars could figure out how to defend against his kick! Tatsu found a friend and mentor in WWE veteran Goldust. After ECW closed, Tatsu was assigned to *Raw*. He was happy to have the chance to compete against some of WWE's biggest stars in *Raw*!

ECW New Superstar Initiative: In 2009, Extreme Championship Wrestling general manager Tiffany announced the New Superstar Initiative. The New Superstar Initiative was a contest that invited wannabe stars to compete in ECW matches. If the competitors could hold their own in the ring, they had the chance to be hired by ECW!

YOSHI TATSU

HEIGHT: 6 feet 1 inch
WEIGHT: 230 pounds
FROM: Gifu, Japan
WWE DEBUT: 2009

ACCOMPLISHMENT:
Winner of
WrestleMania XXVI
26-Man
Battle Royal

Zack Ryder started his WWE career as an "Edge Head"—one of the "Rated R Superstar" Edge's henchmen. After winning the WWE Tag Team Championship with fellow Edge Head Curt Hawkins, Zack became a breakout star in the singles' ranks. His silly costumes and quick comebacks got him noticed in ECW. Now you can catch him on *Raw*, where fans know him as "The Long Island Loudmouth." There's only one thing to say about that: "Woo, woo, woo!"

ZACK RYDER

HEIGHT: 6 feet 1 inch
WEIGHT: 214 pounds
FROM: Long Island, New York
WWE DEBUT: 2007

ACCOMPLISHMENT:
WWE Tag Team Champion

William Regal

An angry ruler can be dangerous. The 2008 King of the Ring, William Regal, definitely proved that point. The former general manager of *Raw* has returned to the ring, joining forces with international talents such as Vladimir Kozlov. Having spent his entire life as a fighter, Regal has a lot of talent in the ring. That, combined with his temper, makes Regal a tough man to defeat.

WILLIAM REGAL

HEIGHT: 6 feet 2 inches
WEIGHT: 240 pounds
FROM: Blackpool, England
WWE DEBUT: 1998

SIGNATURE MOVE:
Regal Stretch

ACCOMPLISHMENTS:
Intercontinental Champion, World Tag Team Champion, European Champion, Hardcore Champion, WCW Television Champion, *Raw* General Manager, King of the Ring (2008)

VLADIMIR KOZLOV

mean Ukrainian grappler Vladimir Kozlov
been a dominant force on the WWE scene
his debut in 2006. At one time, he
allied with William Regal. They were
wn as the Ruthless Roundtable.
e then, he's set out on his own and
made a mark. Kozlov is seen
big threat to his opponents.
esn't matter if he's fighting
enemies on *Raw* or
ckDown—Kozlov knows
of different ways to
t pain on his opponents
likes to use them all in
ring.

VLADIMIR KOZLOV

HEIGHT: 6 feet 8 inches
WEIGHT: 302 pounds
FROM: Moscow, Russia
WWE DEBUT: 2008

SIGNATURE MOVE:
The Iron Curtain

ACCOMPLISHMENT:
WWE Tag Team Champion

Vladimir Kozlov

DARREN YOUNG

Thanks to his funky hairstyle and even funkier moves, Darren Young has brought an excitement to the WWE no fan wants to miss. This exciting rookie has a carefree, laid-back attitude, which makes him a lot different than his former mentor, CM Punk. Young was an original member of Nexus, but was eliminated from that group by John Cena. Young later returned to *NXT* during the show's fifth season, hoping to win a chance for "redemption" on Tuesday nights.

DARREN YOUNG

HEIGHT: 6 feet 1 inch
WEIGHT: 240 pounds
FROM: Miami, Florida
WWE DEBUT: 2010

DAVID OTUNGA

id Otunga is used to living the high life,
he's not afraid to tell you he's better
n you because of it! Before becoming
WWE Superstar, Otunga attended
vard Law School. When he's not
y being a brain, Otunga loves the
z and glam of Hollywood. He is
aged to singer and actress
nifer Hudson and is often seen
king the red carpet at big
ywood events. Despite his
ywood image, Otunga is a
gh, vicious competitor in the
. David Otunga hates to
—something he claims has
er happened in his life! Since
npeting on *NXT*, Otunga has been
owerful force within Nexus.

DAVID OTUNGA

HEIGHT: 6 feet
WEIGHT: 240 pounds
FROM: Hollywood, California
WWE DEBUT: 2010

MICHAEL TARVER

Michael Tarver exploded onto the WWE scene in the inaugural season of *NXT* and was a member of the original Nexus. Tarver is the son of a preacher and has spent his life searching for the same kind of passion he witnessed in his dad. Sports entertainment gave him that passion! Throughout it all, Tarver's dad was there for spiritual and physical guidance—he actually taught his son how to fight! Tarver's father used his experience as one of Mike Tyson's former sparring partners to teach his son how to be a ferocious competitor in the ring. Tarver's star has only risen since leaving Nexus. The WWE Universe is starting to take Tarver's promise to knock out his opponents in two seconds really seriously!

MICHAEL TARVER

HEIGHT: 6 feet 2 inches
WEIGHT: 256 pounds
FROM: Akron, Ohio
WWE DEBUT: 2010

SKIP SHEFFIELD

opposites really attract? Just ask Skip Sheffield.
former mentor, William Regal, is nothing like
m! William Regal is a stuffy, proper Englishman,
ile Sheffield was once known as the "Cornfed
athead." Regal wears robes in the ring, while
effield dons his cowboy hat and vest! Still,
effield learned a lot from Regal's decades of
perience. Sheffield loves a fight and, as a
mer member of the original Nexus,
ks poised to take the WWE
iverse by storm all on his own.

SKIP SHEFFIELD

HEIGHT: 6 feet 2 inches
WEIGHT: 270 pounds
FROM: College Station, Texas
WWE DEBUT: 2010

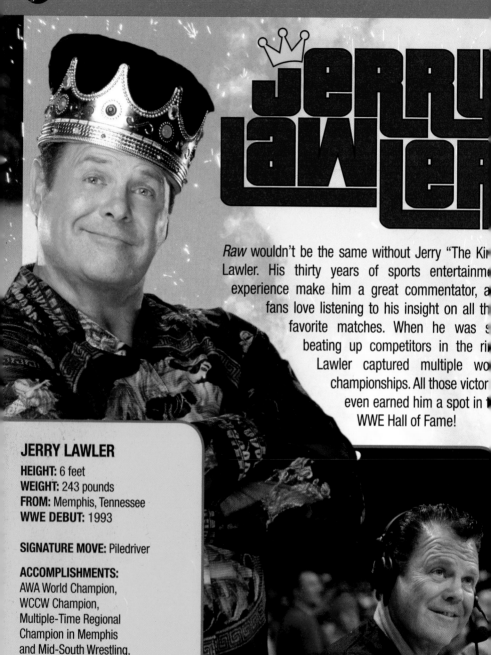

JERRY LAWLER

Raw wouldn't be the same without Jerry "The Kin Lawler. His thirty years of sports entertainm experience make him a great commentator, a fans love listening to his insight on all th favorite matches. When he was s beating up competitors in the ri Lawler captured multiple wo championships. All those victor even earned him a spot in WWE Hall of Fame!

JERRY LAWLER

HEIGHT: 6 feet
WEIGHT: 243 pounds
FROM: Memphis, Tennessee
WWE DEBUT: 1993

SIGNATURE MOVE: Piledriver

ACCOMPLISHMENTS:
AWA World Champion,
WCCW Champion,
Multiple-Time Regional
Champion in Memphis
and Mid-South Wrestling,
WWE Hall of Fame Inductee

"KING"
Jerry Lawler

MICHAEL COLE

ichael Cole has the best seat in the
use. As a commentator, he gets to sit
ngside for tons of WWE matches and
ll all the action in the ring. Cole is
own as the voice of *Raw*—talk
out an awesome job! Before moving
Raw, Cole was the lead announcer
SmackDown.

MICHAEL COLE

HEIGHT: 5 feet 9 inches
WEIGHT: 168 pounds
FROM: Amenia, New York
WWE DEBUT: 1997

ACCOMPLISHMENTS:
Raw Announcer, *SmackDown*
Announcer, Slammy Award
Winner (2009)

MR. McMAHON

MR. McMAHON

HEIGHT: 6 feet 2 inches
WEIGHT: 248 pounds
FROM: Greenwich, Connecticut

ACCOMPLISHMENTS:
Chairman of WWE, WWE
Champion, ECW Champion,
Royal Rumble Winner (1999)

Vincent Kennedy McMahon, or Mr. McMahon as the
Superstars are forced to call him, single-handedly
WWE up from a small New York–based wrestling territc
the billion-dollar global corporation it has become.
a reputation for ruthlessness, Mr. McMahon runs WW
its chairman and owner. He believes that everything he
is right for "business," even though the Superstars an
WWE Universe often disagree with his decisions. If you
him angry, he'll fire you. And he'll enjoy doing it.

It can be very dangerous to mess with the boss. And c
few WWE Superstars have dared challenge Mr. McN
over the years. The WWE chairman has made life in
difficult for Bret "Hit Man" Hart, John Cena, WWE I
Famer "Rowdy" Roddy Piper, Randy Orton, anc
his own son-in-law, Triple H. But no WWE Sup
has been a bigger or longer threat to Mr. McN
than "Stone Cold" Steve Austin. Austin
retired in 2003, hated McMahon and
obeyed his orders. While Austin a
fellow WWE Superstars ofter
the better of Mr. McMaho
chairman knows that he
always get the last laugh.

Going for the Gold: *Raw*'s Championships

In WWE, all the Superstars have one goal: become a champion. In *Raw* alone, there a four championships, and each one has a amazing history. The biggest title in the enti company is the WWE Championship. But the are other titles on *Raw*, too. There's the Unit States Championship, the Divas Championsh and the WWE Tag Team title (the last tw can also be defended on *SmackDown*).

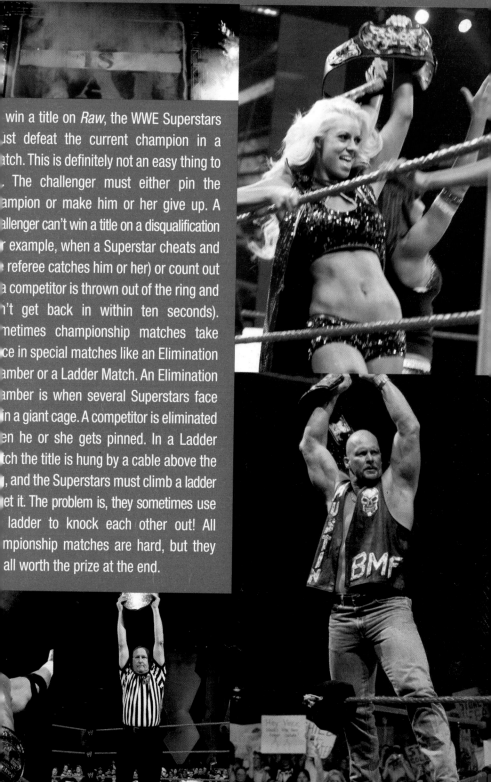

win a title on *Raw*, the WWE Superstars ust defeat the current champion in a atch. This is definitely not an easy thing to . The challenger must either pin the ampion or make him or her give up. A allenger can't win a title on a disqualification r example, when a Superstar cheats and referee catches him or her) or count out a competitor is thrown out of the ring and n't get back in within ten seconds). metimes championship matches take ce in special matches like an Elimination amber or a Ladder Match. An Elimination amber is when several Superstars face in a giant cage. A competitor is eliminated en he or she gets pinned. In a Ladder tch the title is hung by a cable above the , and the Superstars must climb a ladder et it. The problem is, they sometimes use ladder to knock each other out! All mpionship matches are hard, but they all worth the prize at the end.

THE MOST PRECIOUS TITLE...

THE CHAMP

The WWE Championship is the biggest title in all of WW greatest WWE legends have worn the title and shown the that they are the best in the business. Big names who hav the title include Hulk Hogan, "Superstar" Billy Graham Backlund, "Stone Cold" Steve Austin, Triple H, and John All of these champions have had to defend their priz from a never-ending line of challengers. Every WWE Su wants the WWE Championship, and everything he does in out of—the ring is to help him win it.

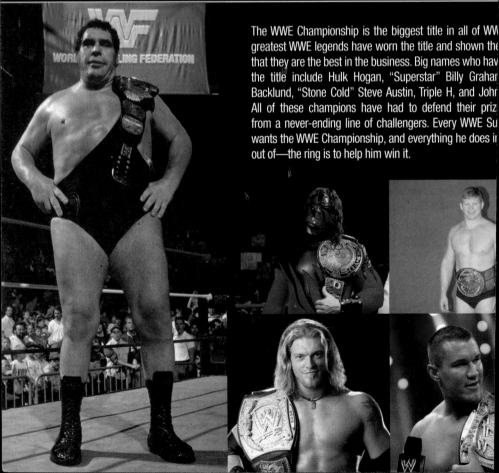

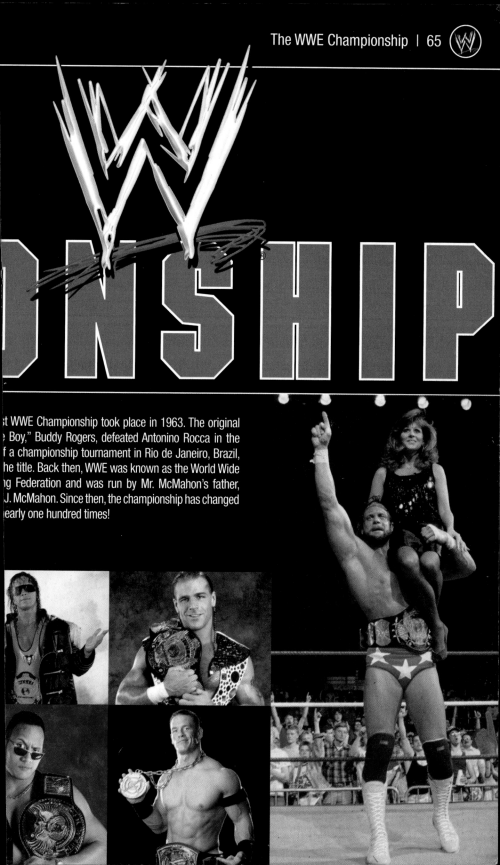

st WWE Championship took place in 1963. The original
Boy," Buddy Rogers, defeated Antonino Rocca in the
f a championship tournament in Rio de Janeiro, Brazil,
he title. Back then, WWE was known as the World Wide
g Federation and was run by Mr. McMahon's father,
J. McMahon. Since then, the championship has changed
early one hundred times!

Photo © Pro Wrestling Illustrated

Photo © Pro Wrestling Illustrated

Former WWE Championship winners include:

Buddy Rogers
Bruno Sammartino
Ivan Koloff
Pedro Morales
Stan Stasiak

"Superstar" Billy Graham
Bob Backlund
The Iron Shiek
Hulk Hogan
André the Giant
Randy "Macho Man" Savage
The Ultimate Warrior
Sgt. Slaughter
Undertaker
Ric Flair
Bret "Hit Man" Hart
Yokozuna

cont'd

Former
WWE Championship
winners include:

Diesel
Shawn Michaels
Sycho Sid
"Stone Cold" Steve Austin
Kane
The Rock
Mankind
Triple H
Mr. McMahon
Big Show
Kurt Angle
Chris Jericho
Brock Lesnar
Eddie Guerrero
JBL
John Cena
Edge
Rob Van Dam
Randy Orton
Jeff Hardy
Batista
Sheamus

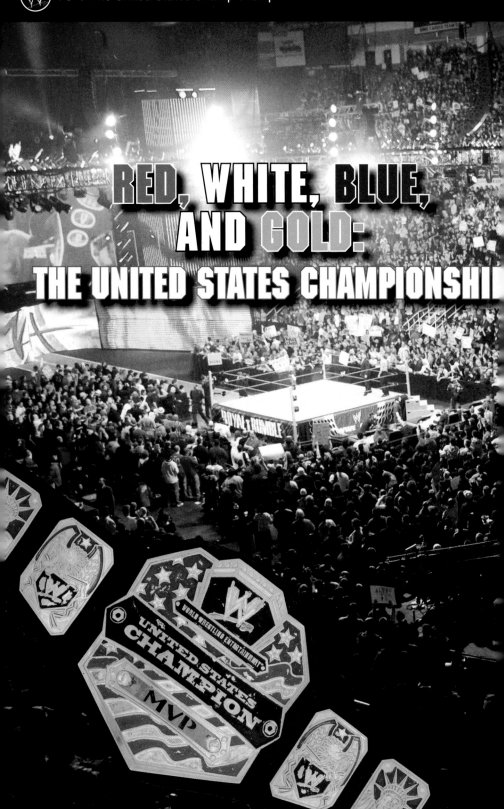

RED, WHITE, BLUE, AND GOLD:
THE UNITED STATES CHAMPIONSHI

at we now know as sports entertainment
an in the mid-1900s when wrestling
moters from around the United States and
ada joined forces to become the National
stling Alliance (NWA). The NWA had its own
of championships, separate from WWE. One
these NWA titles was the United States
mpionship. Whoever held that title was seen
the best competitor in the US. More than
zen WWE Hall of Famers held the United
es Championship title at one time in their
ndary careers.

001, WWE purchased World Championship
stling, which was the last of the old NWA
notions. Because of that, the United States
mpionship was added to the trophies WWE
erstars competed for. Since then, the
has become a first step to the WWE
mpionship. Many of the WWE Superstars
have won the United States Championship
gone on to become the WWE
mpionship winner later in their careers.

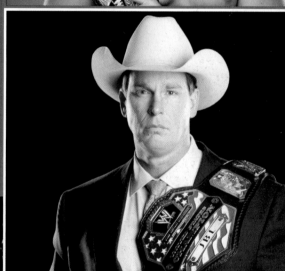

Photo © Pro Wrestling Illustrated

Photo © Pro Wrestling Illustrated

Former United States Championship winners include:

Harley Race
Johnny Valentine
Terry Funk
Paul Jones
Blackjack Mulligan
Bobo Brazil
Ric Flair
Ricky Steamboat
Mr. Wrestling
Jimmy Snuka
Roddy Piper
Wahoo McDaniel
Greg Valentine
Sgt. Slaughter
Magnum T.A.
Dick Slater
Tully Blanchard
Lex Luger
Nikita Koloff

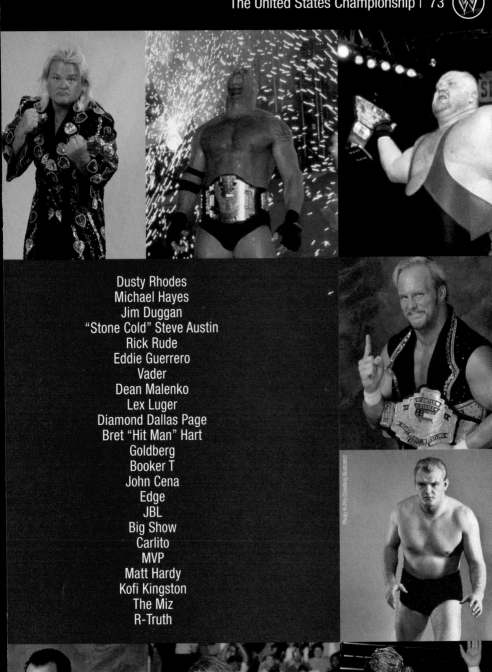

Dusty Rhodes
Michael Hayes
Jim Duggan
"Stone Cold" Steve Austin
Rick Rude
Eddie Guerrero
Vader
Dean Malenko
Lex Luger
Diamond Dallas Page
Bret "Hit Man" Hart
Goldberg
Booker T
John Cena
Edge
JBL
Big Show
Carlito
MVP
Matt Hardy
Kofi Kingston
The Miz
R-Truth

PARTNERS IN PAIN: WWE TAG TEAM CHAMPIONSHIP

team wrestling has a long history in WWE. Over the years, WWE has had two Tag Team
mpionships—the World and WWE. In 2009, the two titles were combined into one Unified
Team Championship. Now the Unified Tag Team Championship is referred to as the WWE Tag
Championship.

Former World and WWE
Tag Team Championship winners include:

The Blackjacks
The Executioners
The Hart Foundation
The Samoans
Natural Disasters
The British Bulldogs
The Road Warriors/Legion of Doom
Demolition
Money, Inc.
D-Generation X

The APA
Rated-RKO
MNM
The Colons
Edge & Christian
The Hardys
Los Guerreros
Legacy
The Hart Dynasty

STRONG & BEAUTIFUL

WWE DIVAS CHAMPIONSHI

The newest title in Unified WWE is the Divas Championship. It was created in 2008 by *SmackDown* general managers Theodore Long and Vickie Guerrero. This new title was an alternative to *Raw*'s Women's Championship. The first Divas Championship match was between Michelle McCool and Natalya. At the end of a grueling battle, McCool came out the winner. She made history as the first WWE Diva to hold the title!

**The WWE Divas
who have held
the title include:**
Melina
Eve
Alicia Fox
Natalya
Michelle McCool
Maryse
Mickie James
Jillian

SMACKDOWN

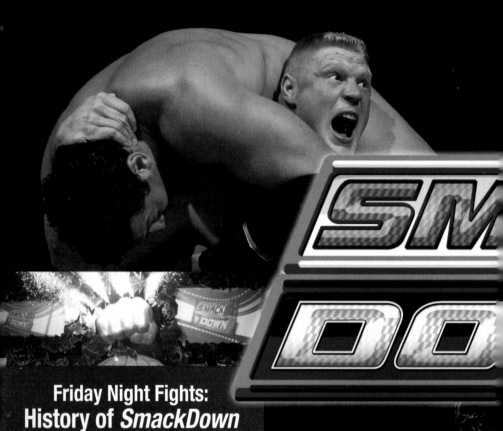

Friday Night Fights:
History of *SmackDown*

WWE has always tried to give its fans what they want. So in August 1999, WWE debuted an exciting new series, *SmackDown*. With Superstar performers like The Rock on the roster, *SmackDown* achieved almost instant success. The show pulled in huge ratings and quickly became the most watched show on its home network. In the decade since then, *SmackDown* has drawn in tons of fans that tune in week after week to see their favorite Superstars and Divas crush one another in the ring.

The show originally aired on Thursday nights and became known to fans everywhere for its wild events and unexpected twists and turns. From Thanksgiving food fights to WWE Championship battles, *SmackDown* was never boring. As the show grew, it attracted some of the biggest names in sports and entertainment. Megastars such as Arnold Schwarzenegger stopped by *SmackDown* to hang out with their favorite WWE legends like "Stone Cold" Steve Austin and The Rock. Thanks to awesome guest stars, intense fights in the ring, and a signature blue color scheme, *SmackDown* established its own identity, separate from other sports entertainment programming.

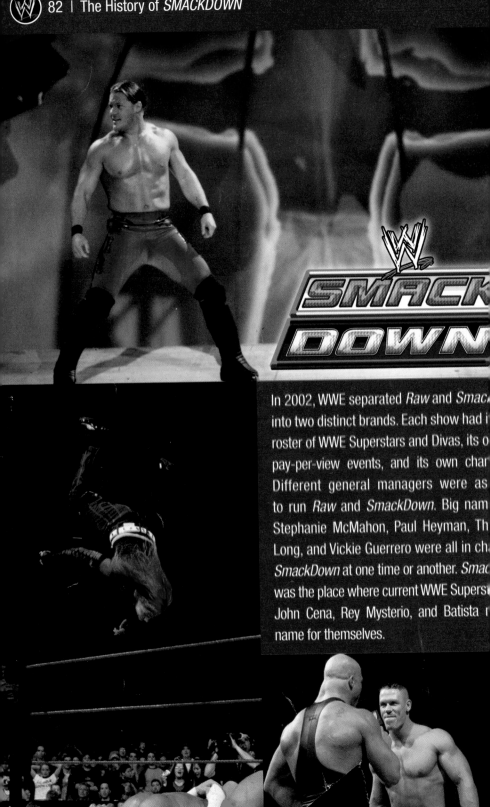

In 2002, WWE separated *Raw* and *Smac*
into two distinct brands. Each show had i
roster of WWE Superstars and Divas, its o
pay-per-view events, and its own char
Different general managers were as
to run *Raw* and *SmackDown*. Big nam
Stephanie McMahon, Paul Heyman, Th
Long, and Vickie Guerrero were all in ch
SmackDown at one time or another. *Smac*
was the place where current WWE Supers
John Cena, Rey Mysterio, and Batista
name for themselves.

2005, *SmackDown* made the move from
ursdays to Fridays. Since then, *Friday Night*
nackDown has become a regular feature at
e end of the week. Fans tune in week after
ek to catch all the action, so *SmackDown*
still the most watched show on its network!
doesn't hurt that *SmackDown* has also
ead to over fifty countries worldwide.
asting some of the greatest Superstars
d Divas in WWE history, *SmackDown* is a
e force in sports entertainment.

Ever since its first episode in 1999, *SmackDown* has introduced the world to a wide variety
talented stars. From intimidating legends like Undertaker and Batista, to fast-rising young st
like Drew McIntyre and Kofi Kingston, *SmackDown* has it all. Every Friday night, these stars sh
off their phenomenal talent and unique skills in the ring. Every *SmackDown* competitor is on
hunt for the World Heavyweight, Intercontinental, and Unified Tag Team Championships, and f
are lucky enough to be along for the ride.

The *SmackDown* Divas are also known for their incredible competitive abilities. Smart, pretty, and powerful, the Divas add a level of class to *SmackDown* that is unmatched anywhere else in sports entertainment. The Diva's Championship is the most sought-after title for the Divas. Whether you like watching the bone-crushing champions do their thing in the ring, or cheering your favorite up-and-coming WWE stars, there's something for everyone to enjoy *SmackDown*. Everyone knows Friday nights are one of the best nights of the week, and the *SmackDown* Superstars and Divas only make it better.

UNDERTAKER

UNDERTAKER

HEIGHT: 6 feet 10½ inches
WEIGHT: 299 pounds
FROM: Death Valley, California
WWE DEBUT: 1990

SIGNATURE MOVES:
Tombstone, Hell's Gate

ACCOMPLISHMENTS: WWE
Champion, World Heavyweight
Champion, World Tag Team
Champion, WCW Tag Team
Champion, Hardcore Champion

Undertaker beats his opponents so badly in the ring, s[...] fans say he even steals their souls! Undertaker has captured nearly every championship in WWE, which is no surprise, since he's been in WWE for twenty years! While fans love Undertaker and have given him the nicknames "The Dead Man" and "The Phenom," opponents fear him. No WWE Superstar is ever the same after going head-to-head with Undertaker! The monster from Death Valley is known in the WWE Universe for his 18–0 streak at WrestleMania, where he's defeated tough fighters like his half brother Kane, Randy Orton, Hall of Famer Jimmy Snuka, and "Mr. WrestleMania" Shawn Michaels.

Undertaker has unique moves in the ring that make him a powerful foe. Over the years, he's mastered some of WWE's toughest matches, like Buried Alive, where the loser is buried under piles of dirt, and the Casket Match, where the only way to win is to get your opponent in a casket. It's rumored that Undertaker is the only man to ever scare WWE chairman Vince McMahon. He even single-handedly forced Shawn Michaels into retirement at WrestleMania XXVI.

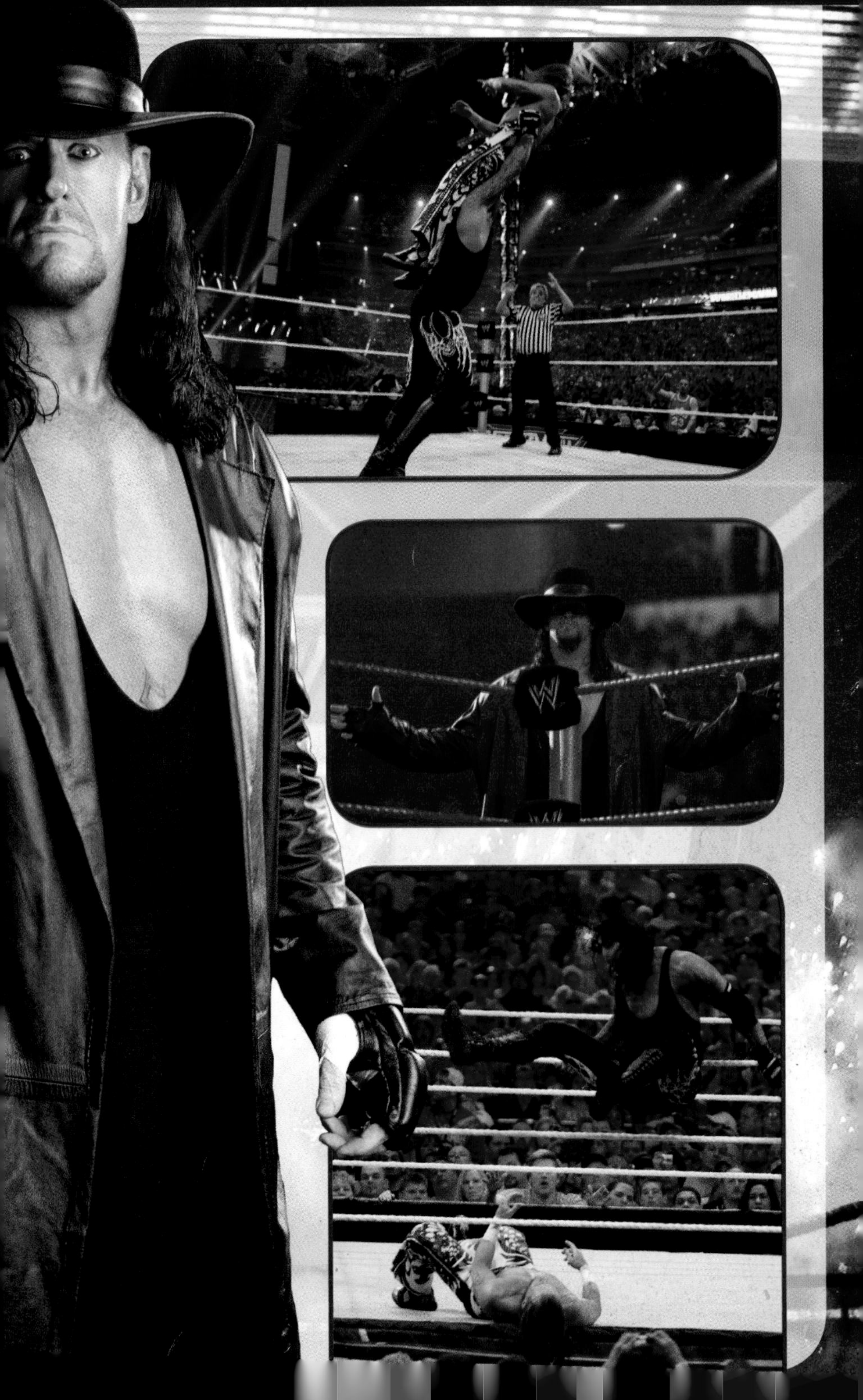

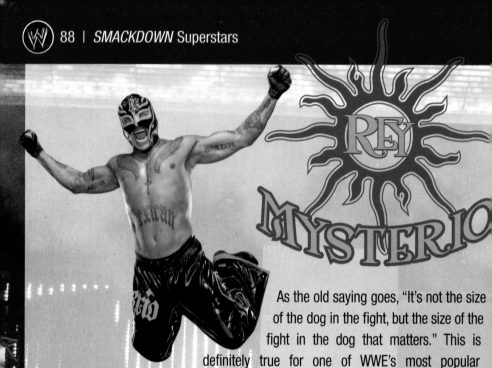

REY MYSTERIO

HEIGHT: 5 feet 6 inches
WEIGHT: 175 pounds
FROM: San Diego, California
WWE DEBUT: 2002

SIGNATURE MOVES:
619, West Coast Pop

ACCOMPLISHMENTS:
World Heavyweight Champion,
Royal Rumble Winner (2006),
Cruiserweight Champion,
WWE Tag Team Champion,
WCW Tag Team Champion,
WCW Cruiserweight
Tag Team Champion,
Intercontinental Champion

As the old saying goes, "It's not the size of the dog in the fight, but the size of the fight in the dog that matters." This is definitely true for one of WWE's most popular Superstars, Rey Mysterio! Rey Mysterio may be one of the smallest competitors in WWE, but he has the heart and the will to win. Thanks to his wild moves in the ring and trademark masks, Rey Mysterio has managed to capture a handful of championships and the imagination of the WWE Universe.

Rey has his amazing airborne moves to thank for his stunning victories in the ring. This has allowed him to defeat opponents twice his size, including giants like the The Great Khali and Big Show. As a former Heavyweight Champion, Rey Mysterio knows just what it to be a champion in WWE.

WADE BARRETT

English rookie Wade Barrett has a l of opinions, and he's not afraid share them with the WW Universe. Barrett, a fierc bare-knuckle brawler, prove he could come out on t as *NXT*'s first winne Barrett didn't take h victory lightly. Durir his first appearanc in the WWE aft capturing the *NX* prize, Barrett forme the Nexus, one of th most dominant groups WWE history. After bein forced out of Nexus by CM Pun Barrett formed a new group, th Corre, taking with him some of his forme Nexus teammates.

WADE BARRETT

HEIGHT: 6 feet 5 inches
WEIGHT: 265 pounds
FROM: Manchester, England
WWE DEBUT: 2010

lk about a sibling rivalry! Kane's
st-ever opponent in WWE was
half brother, Undertaker.
nce then, the brothers have
ced each other in a ton of epic
ttles, like Inferno Matches and
ge Matches. But they've also set
ide their differences to join forces
d become Tag Team Champions!
en though Kane and Undertaker were unstoppable as a
ir, they split up when their personal differences got in
e way once again. But even without his brother, Kane
ts fear in the hearts of his opponents.

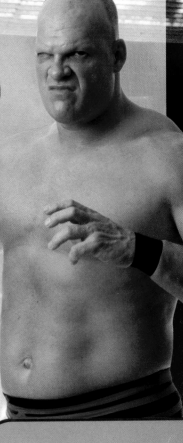

KANE

HEIGHT: 7 feet
WEIGHT: 323 pounds
FROM: Madrid, Spain
WWE DEBUT: 1997

SIGNATURE MOVE: Chokeslam

ACCOMPLISHMENTS:
WWE Champion, World Heavyweight
Champion, ECW Champion,
Intercontinental Champion,
World Tag Team Champion,
WCW Tag Team Champion,
Hardcore Champion

CODY RHODES

Sometimes it can be tough to get out from behind a parent's shadow. It must be *really* tough when your father is WWE Hall of Famer "The American Dream" Dusty Rhodes! Even still, Cody Rhodes has proven himself to be a fierce competitor in WWE. In just a couple years, Cody has surpassed his father to become a WWE Superstar in his own right. Cody became a household name by joining up with Randy Orton's Legacy team, but he split from the group after he established himself as a bona fide Superstar. He now spends his time teaching the WWE Universe how to improve their physical appearance. But don't let his appearance fool you—Rhodes is still a force to be reckoned with in the ring.

CODY RHODES

HEIGHT: 6 feet 1 inch
WEIGHT: 223 pounds
FROM: Charlotte, North Carolina
WWE DEBUT: 2008

ACCOMPLISHMENT:
World Tag Team Champion

KOFi KINGSTON

m! *Boom! Boom!* Kofi Kingston
e WWE Superstar from Ghana,
t Africa, who always seems
ave a smile on his face. Kofi
made an impact on WWE in
hort amount of time by capturing the
rcontinental, United States, and Tag Team
mpionships. His high-impact moves like the
ble in Paradise flying kick make him a threat to
WWE Superstar that challenges him.

KOFI KINGSTON

HEIGHT: 6 feet 1 inch
WEIGHT: 221 pounds
FROM: Ghana, West Africa
WWE DEBUT: 2007

SIGNATURE MOVE:
Trouble in Paradise

ACCOMPLISHMENTS:
Intercontinental Champion, World
Tag Team Champion, United States
Champion

BIG SHOW

BIG SHOW

HEIGHT: 7 feet
WEIGHT: 485 pounds
FROM: Tampa, Florida
WWE DEBUT: 1995

SIGNATURE MOVES:
Chokeslam, Cobra Clutch
Backbreaker

ACCOMPLISHMENTS:
WWE Champion, WCW
Champion, ECW Champion,
World Tag Team Champion,
WWE Hardcore Champion,
United States Champion, Unified
WWE Tag Team Champion

With a name like Big Show, it's no surprise that this WWE Superstar is known for being the largest athlete in WWE—and the world! But Big Show isn't just scary to look at—he's a downright threat in the ring. His size, agility, and smarts in the ring have brought him a lot of success. Big Show has held world championships in every organization he competed in—WWE, WCW, and ECW. Opponents know to cower in fear when Big Show pulls out his left hook or powerful chokeslam. He's a giant—in the ring and out!

...ekiel Jackson grew up in a tough ...ighborhood, where kids had to ...rn from a young age to stand up for ...mselves. Ezekiel learned how to be ...gh and confident, which helped him ...n the last-ever ECW title! After that ...tory, Ezekiel moved to *SmackDown*, ...ere he continues to thrill fans in the ...WE Universe as a prominent and ...minant member of the Corre.

EZEKIEL JACKSON

HEIGHT: 6 feet 4 inches
WEIGHT: 309 pounds
FROM: Harlem, New York
WWE DEBUT: 2008

ACCOMPLISHMENT: Final ECW Champion

Drew McIntyre

Scottish Superstar Drew McIntyre was handpicked by WWE chairman Vince McMahon to join WWE. With that kind of support from the boss, no one was surprised when McIntyre started winning matches. McIntyre is well-known for the vicious rivalry he had with R-Truth that put both Superstars to the test. But despite that, McIntyre captured the Intercontinental Championship after only a few short months on *SmackDown*! McMahon was impressed—and so were all the fans watching from McIntyre's home country!

DREW McINTYRE

HEIGHT: 6 feet 5 inches
WEIGHT: 252 pounds
FROM: Ayr, Scotland
WWE DEBUT: 2009

ACCOMPLISHMENT:
Intercontinental Champion

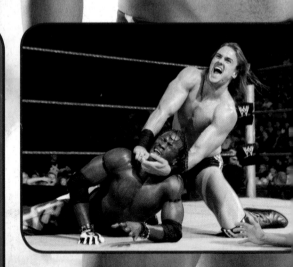

Chavo GUERRERO ™

Mexico and southern Texas, everyone knows the Guerrero name, particularly if they are sports entertainment fans! That's because Chavo Guerrero is a third-generation Superstar with the talent to back up his legacy. Chavo is the nephew of WWE Hall of Famer Eddie Guerrero and grandson of the legendary Gory Guerrero. But Chavo has carved out his own spot in the sports entertainment industry by winning titles and helping to train future Superstars.

CHAVO GUERRERO

HEIGHT: 5 feet 9 inches
WEIGHT: 215 pounds
FROM: El Paso, Texas
WWE DEBUT: 2001

SIGNATURE MOVES:
Gory Bomb, Frog Splash

ACCOMPLISHMENTS:
WCW and WWE Cruiserweight Champion, WWE Tag Team Champion, ECW Champion

Christian

With his fans (or as Christian calls them, "peeps"!) supporting him, Christian return to WWE after a three-year absen In 2009, Christian dominated EC After that, he moved to *Raw* befo being drafted to *SmackDown* 2010. Now fans tune in *SmackDown* to watch Christia incredible talent in the ri It's only a matter of time before t experienced Superstar wins anoth championship.

CHRISTIAN

HEIGHT: 6 feet 2 inches
WEIGHT: 227 pounds
FROM: Toronto, Ontario
WWE DEBUT: 1998

SIGNATURE MOVE:
Killswitch

ACCOMPLISHMENTS:
ECW Champion, Intercontinental Champion, World Tag Team Champion, Light Heavyweight Champion, Hardcore Champion, European Champion

CHRIS MASTERS

Chris Masters, also known as "The Masterpiece," is a rising star in WWE. He is known for his incredible physical strength, particularly when he pulls out his signature move, the "Master Lock," to defeat his opponents! Chris has been a member of several tag teams with WWE Superstars like Carlito, but he has always been able to win matches by himself. Plus, Chris has a warm heart. When smaller Superstars like Hornswoggle have been threatened by opponents, Chris is always ready to step in the ring and offer a little protection. Chris is talented out of the ring, too, and even appeared on the popular Nickelodeon television series *Big Time Rush*!

CHRIS MASTERS

HEIGHT: 6 feet 4 inches
WEIGHT: 275 pounds
FROM: Los Angeles, California
WWE DEBUT: 2005

SIGNATURE MOVE:
The Master Lock

ACCOMPLISHMENT:
Remained undefeated in Master Lock Challenges for over two years—no one was able to break out of his Master Lock hold.

ROSA mendes

Any WWE fan would love to meet their favorite s
and learn all about how to be a fierce competi
from them. For Rosa Mendes, this dream actua
came true! Before coming to WWE, Rosa w
obsessed with The Glamazon Beth Phoenix
fact, she was such a fan that she followed *R*
from city to city just so she could watch
favorite Diva in action! The Glamaz
appreciated Rosa's support and eventua
pulled her out from the crowd. Beth tau
Rosa everything she knew about WV
Rosa already had the passion; now she
the know-how, too. That was enough
convince WWE to hire Rosa as a Diva!

ROSA MENDES
HEIGHT: 5 feet 8 inches
FROM: San Mateo, California
WWE DEBUT: 2008

Rosa Mendes

HORNSWOGGLE

...rnswoggle might be small in size, but he's ...g in talent, heart, and determination—all ...portant qualities to be a success in the ring! ...e unique competitor is known for his pranks, ...kes, and the way he tortures any WWE Superstar ...at crosses his path. Hornswoggle was once ...lieved to be the son of Mr. McMahon, though it ...rned out not to be true. Since then, Hornswoggle ...s aligned himself with D-Generation X as their ...ascot. When he's not pulling pranks on the other ...rformers in the locker room, Hornswoggle ... dominating the ring. He even captured the ...uiserweight Championship!

HORNSWOGGLE

HEIGHT: 4 feet 4 inches
WEIGHT: 129 pounds
FROM: Dublin, Ireland
WWE DEBUT: 2006

SIGNATURE MOVE: Tadpole Splash

ACCOMPLISHMENT:
Cruiserweight Champion

JACK SWAGGER

Jack "The All-American American" Swagger brought his success as a wrestler at the University of Oklahoma to WWE in 2008. After winning an ECW championship, Swagger decided to take it to the next level by joining *Raw*. Known for dropping down to do push-ups before his matches, Swagger has shown that he has the confidence and skills needed to succeed in WWE—success that includes winning Money in the Bank at WrestleMania XXVI and cashing in his contract to win the World Heavyweight Championship five days later!

JACK SWAGGER

HEIGHT: 6 feet 6 inches
WEIGHT: 263 pounds
FROM: Perry, Oklahoma
WWE DEBUT: 2008

SIGNATURE MOVE:
Gutwrench Powerbomb

ACCOMPLISHMENTS:
World Heavyweight Champion, ECW Champion, Money in the Bank Winner

Kelly Kelly ™

The WWE Divas are popular throughout the WWE Universe because of the way they combine beauty and toughness. Kelly Kelly is no exception. During her career in WWE, Kelly Kelly has proven herself to be a force in the ring. It wasn't always easy for her, though. In the beginning, fans only knew her as Mike Knox's girlfriend! Even though she hasn't won a Women's or Divas Championship yet, Kelly Kelly continues to improve. And someday soon, the female champions in WWE are going to find out just how far she's come.

KELLY KELLY

HEIGHT: 5 feet 5 inches
FROM: Jacksonville, Florida
WWE DEBUT: 2006

HAWKINS

Curt Hawkins started his career in WWE in the best way possible: as a protégé, or follower, to the "Ultimate Opportunist" Edge! Together, Hawkins and Zack Ryder protected Edge from enemy attacks, which even involved dressing up and pretending to be Edge more than once! The so-called "Edge Heads" won the World Tag Team Championship before splitting from Edge—and from each other. Since then, Hawkins hasn't had the same kind of success, but he's still trying to work his way to the top of the *SmackDown* rankings.

CURT HAWKINS

HEIGHT: 6 feet 1 inch
WEIGHT: 221 pounds
FROM: Long Island, New York
WWE DEBUT: 2007

ACCOMPLISHMENT: World Tag Team Championship

DOLPH ZIGGLER

If you haven't heard of Dolph Ziggler yet, then you just haven't been paying attention! This cocky young Superstar has made it his goal to personally introduce himself to everyone in the WWE Universe. But despite his attitude, there is no denying that Ziggler is a talented up-and-comer with the strength to do some serious damage in WWE. Plus, he believes so strongly in himself that it's hard for others not to believe in him, too! Ziggler was once romantically linked to WWE Diva Maria, but he ended their relationship when he decided to put all his focus on his goal of someday winning the Intercontinental Championship. Currently, Ziggler has joined forces with a new romantic interest: *SmackDown* adviser Vickie Guerrero.

DOLPH ZIGGLER

HEIGHT: 6 feet
WEIGHT: 221 pounds
FROM: Hollywood, Florida
WWE DEBUT: 2008

ACCOMPLISHMENTS: World Tag Team Champion, Intercontinental Champion, World Heavyweight Champion

JTG

It can be tough growing up in a big city like Brooklyn, New York. Just ask JTG—that's where he was born. JTG used to make up one half of the tag team Cryme Tyme, along with his ex-partner, Shad. Shad and JTG actually grew up together. When they made it to WWE in 2006, they felt like they'd accomplished their dream. But Cryme Tyme split in 2010 when Shad left after JTG didn't save him from losing a match. Now JTG has set out to make a name for himself, by himself.

JTG
HEIGHT: 6 feet 1 inch
WEIGHT: 235 pounds
FROM: Brooklyn, New York
WWE DEBUT: 2006

BETH PHOENIX

The Glamazon Beth Phoenix has proven just how tough a WWE Diva can be. She is ruthless in the ring and loves pulling out her signature set of moves on her opponents, like her missiledropkick and the "Glam Slam" bodyslam. Beth has dominated the WWE Divas division since her debut in 2006. She won her first WWE Women's Championship in 2007. In 2010, she made history by being the second woman ever to enter the Royal Rumble! Beth gets people talking *outside* the ring, too. For a brief period of time, The Glamazon was romantically linked to Santino Marella, but their relationship ended when she was traded from *Raw* to *SmackDown*.

BETH PHOENIX

HEIGHT: 5 feet 7 inches
FROM: Buffalo, New York
WWE DEBUT: 2006

ACCOMPLISHMENTS:
WWE Women's Champion,
Royal Rumble Entrant (2010)

Layla™

When Layla entered the 2006 WWE Diva Search competition, she had no idea what life would really be like as a WWE Diva. She knew the WWE Divas were intense competitors, but she had no idea *how* intense. Layla discovered just how strong her fellow Divas were when she got the chance to square off against them in the ring. Layla was born in London, England, and once danced for the Miami Heat in the NBA. After that, she was a dancer in ECW. Since leaving ECW and joining *SmackDown*, Layla has proven herself to be more than just a dancer—she won the Women's Championship!

LAYLA

HEIGHT: 5 feet 2 inches
FROM: London, England
WWE DEBUT: 2006

ACCOMPLISHMENTS:
Women's Champion, Winner of the 2006 $250,000 Diva Search

michelle McCOOL ™

Even when she was a school teacher, Michelle McCool had a love for the world of sports entertainment. As a kid growing up in Florida, she went to sports entertainment events with her father and grandfather. She idolized WWE Hall of Famer "The American Dream" Dusty Rhodes. Michelle's dream came true in 2004 when she joined WWE. It was a feat that could be topped only by her performance as the first-ever Diva's Champion in 2008! Michelle made history again by winning the WWE Women's Championship the following year. That victory made her the first woman to hold both titles!

MICHELLE McCOOL

HEIGHT: 5 feet 10 inches
FROM: Palatka, Florida
WWE DEBUT: 2004

ACCOMPLISHMENTS:
First Diva's Champion, WWE Women's Champion, Winner of the 2008 *SmackDown* Top Diva Competition

xoxo

HEATH SLATER

There's no rookie/pro partnership in *NXT* history that worked as well as the one between Heath Slater, the "Rock Band without Instruments," and "Captain Charisma" Christian. Their personalities meshed well together, and their friendship led to great success in the ring. Like his fellow *NXT* rookies, Slater was a member of the original Nexus. He remained loyal to former Nexus leader Wade Barrett and joined the Corre, Barrett's new group. Alongside fellow Corre member Justin Gabriel, Slater has risen quickly to the top of the WWE, capturing the WWE Tag Team Championship.

HEATH SLATER

HEIGHT: 6 feet 2 inches
WEIGHT: 230 pounds
FROM: Pineville, West Virginia
WWE DEBUT: 2010

ACCOMPLISHMENT: WWE Tag Team Champion

Heath Slater

JUSTIN GABRIEL

The rookie from Cape Town, South Africa, already has a ton of talent and charisma, and it's taken him to the top of the WWE. Less than a year after joining the WWE, Justin and partner Heath Slater captured the WWE Tag Team Championship. Justin is known for his purity, passion, and goodness. He has fought for everything he's gotten in his life and is no stranger to adversity. He sees the challenges of WWE as just another obstacle to overcome. A former member of the original Nexus, Gabriel has become a powerful member of the Corre on *SmackDown*.

JUSTIN GABRIEL

HEIGHT: 6 feet 1 inch
WEIGHT: 215 pounds
FROM: Cape Town, South Africa
WWE DEBUT: 2010

ACCOMPLISHMENT: WWE Tag Team Champion

FINLAY

Finlay grew up in Ireland, where he became an expert in wrestling and boxing. He won several championships in Europe before joining WCW in 1995 and eventually WWE in 2004. With his trusty shillelagh always in his hand, the tough Irishman has defeated many WWE Superstars, which has earned him respect—in the WWE locker room and everywhere else in the WWE Universe. Scrappy Finlay loves a fight, and never ever backs down from his opponents.

FINLAY

HEIGHT: 6 feet 2 inches
WEIGHT: 233 pounds
FROM: Belfast, Northern Ireland
WWE DEBUT: 2004

SIGNATURE MOVE: The Celtic Cross

ACCOMPLISHMENTS:
United States Champion, WCW Television Champion, WCW Hardcore Champion

TRENT BARRETA

rent Barreta first got noticed in WWE thanks to ECW eneral manager Tiffany's New Superstar Initiative. ven though he was one half of a tag team with aylen Croft, Barreta made it his personal goal to e the best to ever come out of Tiffany's talent ecruitment. Once ECW closed in 2010, arreta joined his fist-bumping partner, Croft, n *SmackDown* as determined as ever to rove that he's the best Superstar in WWE.

TRENT BARRETA

HEIGHT: 6 feet 1 inch
WEIGHT: 230 pounds
FROM: Mount Sinai, New York
WWE DEBUT: 2010

THEODORE LONG

Theodore Long has had many jobs throughout his thirty-year career in sports entertainment. He's been a manager, a referee, and even an in-ring competitor! But he has found his greatest success as the general manager of *SmackDown*. During his time on the Friday night brand, Long has engineered explosive trades and booked very high-profile main events. While some, including Mr. McMahon, have been critical of Long's work, he never quits trying to make *SmackDown* the best show on TV. Holla, player!

THEODORE LONG

HEIGHT: 5 feet 10 inches
WEIGHT: 163 pounds
FROM: Atlanta, Georgia

ACCOMPLISHMENTS:
General Manager of *SmackDown*,
General Manager of ECW

VICKIE GUERRERO

With her shrill "Excuse me!" Vickie Guerrero demands respect from the WWE Universe—but she rarely gets it! The former general manager of both *Raw* and *SmackDown* has earned her reputation by stacking the deck against some of the WWE's most popular Superstars. She puts them in matches that seem impossible to win, often as an act of revenge! Even though she is no longer *SmackDown*'s general manager, Vickie still serves as a consultant to Theodore Long.

VICKIE GUERRERO

HEIGHT: 5 feet 6 inches
FROM: El Paso, Texas

ACCOMPLISHMENTS:
Raw General Manager,
SmackDown General Manager,
Miss WrestleMania, Official
Consultant to *SmackDown*

TODD GRISHAM

The WWE Universe has really come to know Todd Grisham, thanks to the many jobs he's had over the years. Todd has been a backstage interviewer on *Raw*, *SmackDown*, and many big pay-per view events. He was the lead announcer o ECW before taking over for WWE Hall of Fame Jim Ross (who was out due to illness) behind the microphone on *SmackDown*. Thanks to hi deep knowledge of the world of sport entertainment, Todd Grisham adds a lot to th WWE Universe's *SmackDown* experience.

TODD GRISHAM

HEIGHT: 6 feet 1 inch
WEIGHT: 160 pounds
FROM: Bay Minette, Alabama

ACCOMPLISHMENTS:
SmackDown Play-by-Play Announcer,
ECW Play-by-Play Announcer

Matt Striker

...riker was once a New York City high school ...acher. Then he found a new "classroom"— ...e ECW ring! Unfortunately, Striker ...dn't have much success there, and ...er a series of defeats he retired from ...mpetition—though he did find great ...ccess after that as an announcer on ...W. He later moved onto *SmackDown*, ...ere he called matches alongside ...WE Hall of Famer Jim Ross and current ...ay-by-play man Todd Grisham. Striker ...n also be seen as the host of *NXT*.

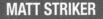

MATT STRIKER

HEIGHT: 5 feet 10 inches
WEIGHT: 224 pounds
FROM: Bayside, New York

ACCOMPLISHMENTS:
ECW Commentator, *SmackDown*
Commentator, Host of *WWE NXT*

Friday Night Gold: The *SmackDown* Championships

SmackDown is where the WWE Universe goes on Friday nights for the best in-ring competition. That competition boils down to the three WWE championships that can only be won or defended on *SmackDown*. Some of the longest lasting titles in sports entertainment history can be found on *SmackDown*, including the World Heavyweight Championship, the Intercontinental Title, and the Women's Championship. The current WWE Superstars and Divas all want to add their names to that impressive list of champs.

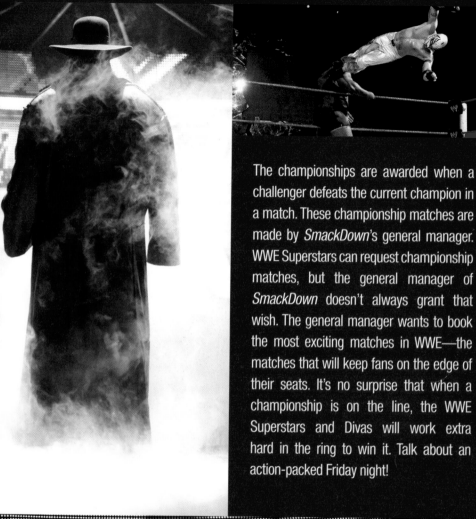

The championships are awarded when a challenger defeats the current champion in a match. These championship matches are made by *SmackDown*'s general manager. WWE Superstars can request championship matches, but the general manager of *SmackDown* doesn't always grant that wish. The general manager wants to book the most exciting matches in WWE—the matches that will keep fans on the edge of their seats. It's no surprise that when a championship is on the line, the WWE Superstars and Divas will work extra hard in the ring to win it. Talk about an action-packed Friday night!

THE OLDEST PRIZE IN WRESTLING

HEAVYWEIGHT

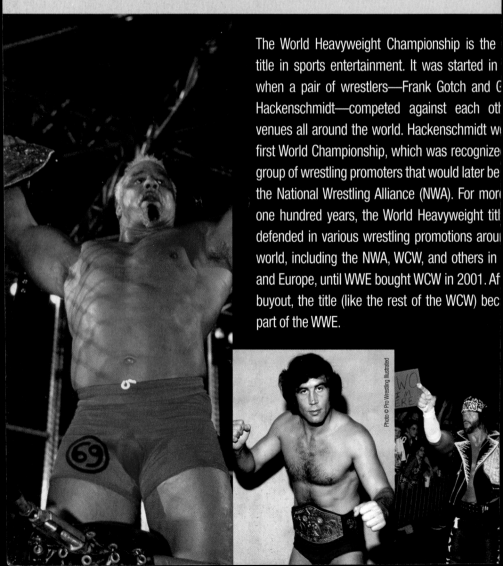

The World Heavyweight Championship is the title in sports entertainment. It was started in when a pair of wrestlers—Frank Gotch and G Hackenschmidt—competed against each oth venues all around the world. Hackenschmidt w first World Championship, which was recognize group of wrestling promoters that would later be the National Wrestling Alliance (NWA). For mor one hundred years, the World Heavyweight titl defended in various wrestling promotions arou world, including the NWA, WCW, and others in and Europe, until WWE bought WCW in 2001. Af buyout, the title (like the rest of the WCW) bec part of the WWE.

Photo © Pro Wrestling Illustrated

HE WORLD CHAMPIONSHIP

its long history, the World Heavyweight
pionship has been held by icons like "The
can Dream" Dusty Rhodes, the Funk brothers,
Brisco, Kerry Von Erich, Ron Simmons (the first
n American champion), Bret Hart, The Rock,
H, John Cena, and Undertaker. It is the only
headline both WrestleMania (WWE's biggest
and Starrcade (NWA/WCW's biggest event). Its
ge and tradition is unmatched. It is the biggest
on *SmackDown*.

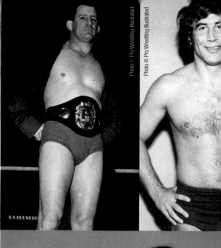

Former World Heavyweight Championship winners include:

George Hackenschmidt
Frank Gotch
Pat O'Conner

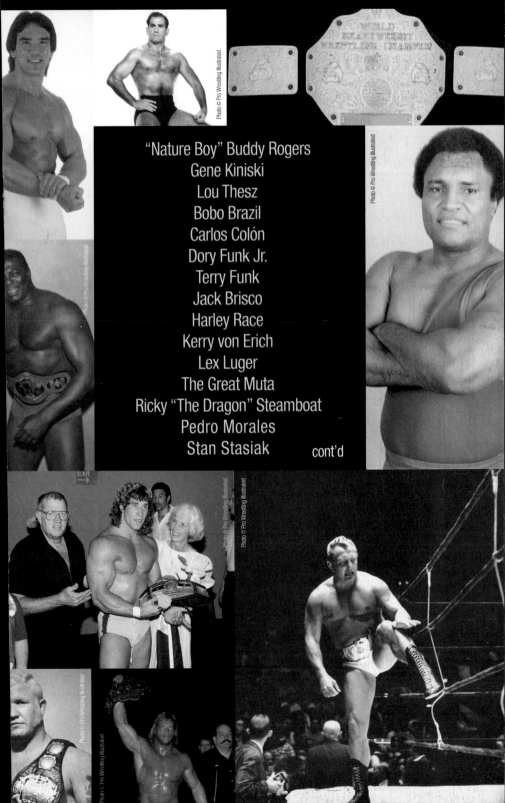

"Nature Boy" Buddy Rogers
Gene Kiniski
Lou Thesz
Bobo Brazil
Carlos Colón
Dory Funk Jr.
Terry Funk
Jack Brisco
Harley Race
Kerry von Erich
Lex Luger
The Great Muta
Ricky "The Dragon" Steamboat
Pedro Morales
Stan Stasiak   cont'd

Former World Heavyweight Championship winners include:

Big Show (then known as the Giant)
Randy "Macho Man" Savage
Bret "Hit Man" Hart
Scott Steiner
Triple H
Randy Orton
Shawn Michaels
Undertaker
Chris Jericho
John Cena
Great Khali
Batista
Edge
CM Punk
Rey Mysterio
Batista

THE INTERCONTINENTA

In 1979, the World Wide Wrestling Federation—which is what WWE was called then—crowne Patterson the first ever Intercontinental Champion. Patterson won the new title in Rio de Ja Brazil. Since then, the Intercontinental Championship has been held by the some of the talented WWE Superstars ever! Winning the Intercontinental Championship is also a sign tha career is headed for great things. The World Champions of tomorrow are often the Interconti Champions of today.

A TITLE FO THE ELITE

HAMPIONSHIP

al WWE Hall of Fame inductees were once Intercontinental Champions. The title has a history
t as impressive as the WWE and World Heavyweight Championships. Current WWE Superstar
Jericho holds the record for most Intercontinental reigns (nine), though the Honky Tonk Man
e championship for the longest period of time (fourteen months). In 1999, former Diva Chyna
he the only woman to ever win the title! There have been many amazing technical matches for
ampionship. Fans still remember those incredible events!

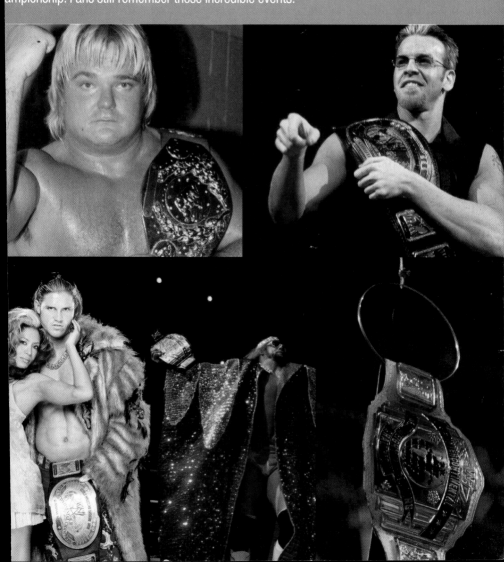

Former Intercontinental Championship winners include:

Pat Patterson
Ken Patera
Don Muraco
Pedro Morales
Tito Santana
Honky Tonk Man
Greg Valentine
Randy "Macho Man" Savage
Ricky "The Dragon" Steamboat
"Ravishing" Rick Rude
"Mr. Perfect" Curt Hennig
Kerry von Erich

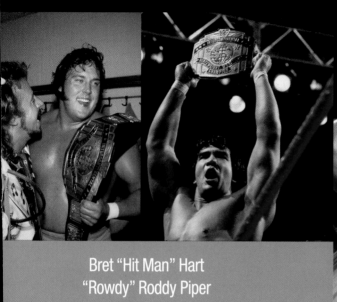

Bret "Hit Man" Hart
"Rowdy" Roddy Piper
Shawn Michaels
"Stone Cold" Steve Austin
The Rock
Goldust
Triple H
Edge
Chris Jericho
Chyna
Shelton Benjamin
Christian
Kane
John Morrison
Drew McIntyre

LADIES' FIRST TITLE

THE WWE WOMEN'S CHAMPIONSHIP

The WWE Superstars' titles aren't the only ones with impressive histories. The WWE Divas also compete for a legendary title. The first WWE Women's Championship was in 1956 and was won by WWE Hall of Famer the Fabulous Moolah. Moolah held the championship for twenty-eight years! Talk about an incredible winning streak! Moolah's streak was broken when she lost to 2010 Hall of Fame inductee Wendi Richter. Today, the WWE Divas give it their all in the ring in hopes of being crowned the next Women's Champion.

Former Women's Championship winners include:

The Fabulous Moolah

Wendi Richter

Lelani Kai

Alundra Blayze

Trish Stratus

Chyna

Stephanie McMahon

Lita

"Glamazon" Beth Phoenix

Mickie James

Michelle McCool

GONE BUT NOT FORGOTTEN: RETIRED WWE CHAMPIONSHIP

There are currently six championships the Superstars and Divas compete for on _____ and *SmackDown*. But there are also a few titles that have been retired. Even though ___ championships were only around for a short while, they were held by big name Superstars.

ECW

The ECW Championship began in a sr____ Philadelphia promotion known for its extre____ action. WWE bought ECW and continued ____ championship until 2010. The first E_____ Champion was Jimmy Snuka, and the last ____ Ezekiel Jackson.

Other notable ECW Championsh___ winners include:

Tommy Dreamer

Sabu

Big Show

Christian

Kane

Jack Swagger

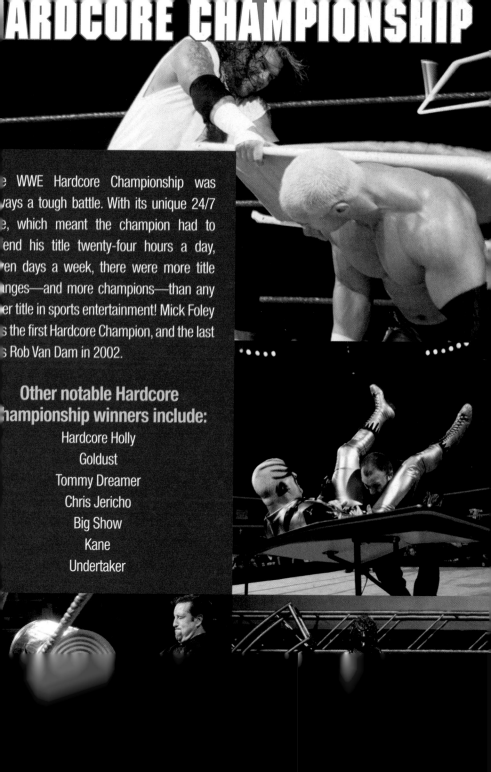

ARDCORE CHAMPIONSHIP

e WWE Hardcore Championship was
vays a tough battle. With its unique 24/7
e, which meant the champion had to
end his title twenty-four hours a day,
en days a week, there were more title
anges—and more champions—than any
er title in sports entertainment! Mick Foley
s the first Hardcore Champion, and the last
s Rob Van Dam in 2002.

Other notable Hardcore Championship winners include:

Hardcore Holly
Goldust
Tommy Dreamer
Chris Jericho
Big Show
Kane
Undertaker

EUROPEAN CHAMPIONSHIP

In the late 1990s, WWE created a new European Championship. The first champion was "The British Bulldog" Davey Boy Smith, who defended his title around the world, not just in Europe. For five years, WWE Superstars battled each other for the title until Jeff Hardy captured it for the final time in 2002.

Other notable European Championship winners include:

Shawn Michaels

Triple H

Mark Henry

William Regal

LIGHT HEAVYWEIGHT AND CRUISERWEIGHT CHAMPIONSHIPS

Although WWE is known for being a land of giants with its supersized Superstars, a group of smaller wrestlers, known as light heavyweights or cruiserweights, once competed in their own division for their own championships. WWE had the Light Heavyweight Championship and the first winner was Taka Michinoku. WCW had a cruiserweight title that was first held by Brian Pillman. When WWE purchased WCW, the two titles were combined into the WWE Cruiserweight Championship. Hornswoggle was the final Cruiserweight Championship titleholder.

Other notable Light Heavyweight and Cruiserweight Championship winners include:

Eddie Guerrero

Matt Hardy

Rey Mysterio

Chris Jericho

Dean Malenko

Tajiri

THE NEW TALENT OF NXT

n February 2010, WWE Chairman Mr. McMahon announced the debut of the next evolution of sports entertainment. Mr. McMahon promised to give the WWE Universe a new program that would be exciting and intriguing. He revealed that the new program would be called *NXT*. *NXT* introduces aspiring WWE Superstars to the WWE Universe. But it is more than just an hour of high-flying sports entertainment action—it's also a competition! Eight young, hungry WWE rookies are given the opportunity to fight it out in the ring for the chance to be the next big Superstar.

Each rookie is given a mentor. And what better mentor than a current WWE Superstar? Some of these rookie/pro combinations have worked out well, like Christian and Heath Slater's pairing. In these cases, the pro has been able to help the young rookie's career. But other matchups have been disastrous, like The Miz and Daniel Bryan. The pros are the ones who vote for the rookie they think should win the WWE talent contract, but no one is allowed to vote for or against their assigned rookie.

NXT rookies are judged on their wins and losses, the strength of their opponents, their work ethic, whether they have the "it" factor. The *NXT* pros get together every few weeks to cast their votes. ugh the win/loss record can't be argued—either the rookie lost the match or won—the rest of andards for votes are all a matter of opinion. The votes result in a list of rankings for the *NXT* rookies. few weeks, the lowest ranking rookie is eliminated. The *NXT* rookies all work very hard to stay alive competition. The WWE Universe has to tune in every week to find out who is going home next!

NXT
SEASON TWO

The first season of *NXT* proved so popular that a new group of rookies was brought in to compete for another coveted spot on a WWE roster. Like their predecessors, these eight rookies were partnered with WWE Superstars who acted as their mentors. This second season group has a lot to prove to the WWE Universe. They're all determined to prove themselves to their pros, their fans, and especially to themselves. They claim to be more talented than the original group of rookies, and they believe they will prove to be the most dominant force in WWE.

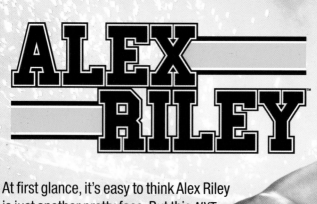

ALEX RILEY

At first glance, it's easy to think Alex Riley is just another pretty face. But this *NXT* rookie is so much more than that. He has degrees in economics and communications from Boston College, and he uses his education to outthink his opponents in the ring. Thanks to the help from his pro, The Miz, Alex Riley has proven to be a fierce competitor with a great chance at winning the competition. And no matter what happens in the ring, Riley always looks good while doing it.

ALEX RILEY
HEIGHT: 6 feet 2 inches
WEIGHT: 240 pounds
FROM: Georgetown, Virginia

WWE PRO: The Miz

ELI COTTONWOOD

is massive monster uses his impressive size to battle s way through the other *NXT* rookies to the top of the nkings. An accomplished athlete, Cottonwood played ofessional basketball for the NBA's Milwaukee Bucks d was even a basketball coach for the University of sconsin. But the WWE ring is very different from a sketball court. Luckily for Cottonwood, he's proven at he's up to the challenge. And with the "Shaman Sexy" John Morrison as his pro, Eli Cottonwood sure to succeed.

ELI COTTONWOOD

HEIGHT: 7 feet
WEIGHT: 313 pounds
FROM: River Falls, Wisconsin

WWE PRO: John Morrison

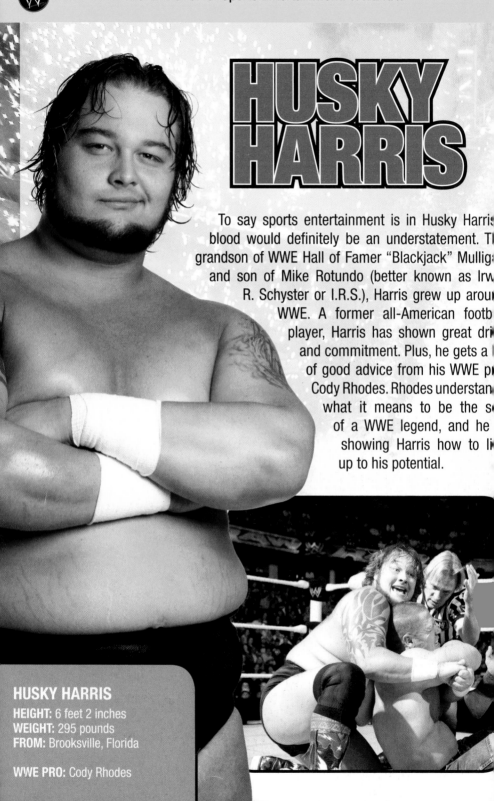

HUSKY HARRIS

To say sports entertainment is in Husky Harris' blood would definitely be an understatement. The grandson of WWE Hall of Famer "Blackjack" Mulligan and son of Mike Rotundo (better known as Irwin R. Schyster or I.R.S.), Harris grew up around WWE. A former all-American football player, Harris has shown great drive and commitment. Plus, he gets a lot of good advice from his WWE pro, Cody Rhodes. Rhodes understands what it means to be the son of a WWE legend, and he's showing Harris how to live up to his potential.

HUSKY HARRIS
HEIGHT: 6 feet 2 inches
WEIGHT: 295 pounds
FROM: Brooksville, Florida

WWE PRO: Cody Rhodes

r the first time in *NXT* history, a rookie
s placed with a pair of WWE Divas as
pros. These weren't just any Divas,
ugh. Kaval's mentors, Layla and
chelle McCool, were the coholders of
WWE Women's Championship. Plus,
val is an experienced athlete himself.
worked in sports entertainment
mpanies all over the world, but none
big or as well-known as WWE. His
iding Divas were determined to prove
t they can make him a winner and a
ampion, just like they are.

KAVAL
HEIGHT: 5 feet 7 inches
WEIGHT: 175 pounds
FROM: Brooklyn, New York

WWE PROS: Layla and
Michelle McCool

LUCKY CANNON

You could argue that Lucky Cannon has more enthusiasm and appreciation for life than any other WWE Superstar! As a boy, he had a near-death experience—but he survived. Since then, he's decided to make the most of his life, no matter the circumstances. Cannon knows that every minute is important and should be lived to the fullest. He works hard to make the very best of every opportunity and experience he gets. With Mark Henry as his pro, it shouldn't be too hard to make the best out of this amazing opportunity.

LUCKY CANNON
HEIGHT: 6 feet 5 inches
WEIGHT: 238 pounds
FROM: New Port Ritchey, Florida

WWE PRO: Mark Henry

MICHAEL McGILLICUTTY

Michael McGillicutty has a lot to live up to. His grandfather, Larry "The Axe" Hennig, was a legend of the ring in the 1950s and 1960s. Mike's dad is WWE Hall of Famer "Mr. Perfect" Curt Hennig. With a heritage like that, there are a lot of expectations for greatness in the ring. So far, McGillicutty has lived up to all the expectations and shown that like his father he is pretty much "absolutely perfect."

MICHAEL McGILLICUTTY
HEIGHT: 6 feet 3 inches
WEIGHT: 224 pounds
FROM: Champlin, Minnesota

WWE PRO: Kofi Kingston

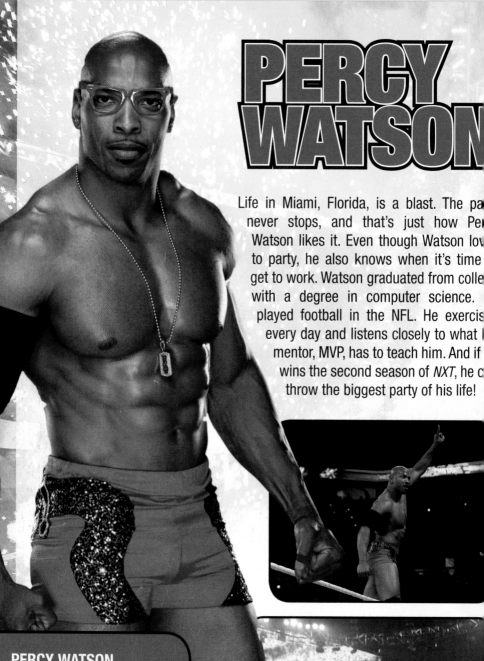

PERCY WATSON

Life in Miami, Florida, is a blast. The pa
never stops, and that's just how Pe
Watson likes it. Even though Watson lov
to party, he also knows when it's time
get to work. Watson graduated from colle
with a degree in computer science.
played football in the NFL. He exercis
every day and listens closely to what I
mentor, MVP, has to teach him. And if
wins the second season of *NXT*, he c
throw the biggest party of his life!

PERCY WATSON
HEIGHT: 6 feet 3 inches
WEIGHT: 235 pounds
FROM: Miami, Florida

WWE PRO: MVP

TITUS O'NEIL

here's nothing Titus O'Neil enjoys ore than competition. He feels ght at home in WWE as one of the *XT* rookies. He played college and rofessional football, but his love for ompetition goes beyond athletics. e has worked on several political ampaigns, including a job as staffer during the 2008 US residential campaign. With so uch passion for victory, Titus has good chance of winning *NXT* and king over the whole WWE.

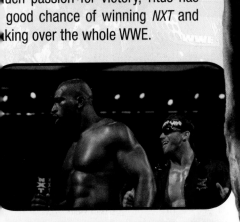

TITUS O'NEIL

HEIGHT: 6 feet 4 inches
WEIGHT: 267 pounds
FROM: Live Oak, Florida

WWE PRO: Zack Ryder

THE BIGGES

PAY-PE

For more than twenty-five years, WWE has put on the biggest events in sports entertain
These events are held on pay-per-view, which means that viewers have to pay their cable or sa
companies to watch. These big events feature matches where Superstars go head to he
hopes of winning a championship or settling an old disagreement. These events aren't your star
run-of-the-mill wrestling matches—far from it! WWE gets creative with their pay-per-view e
like holding the match inside a steel cage! Pay-per-view matches are even more intense
action-packed than the matches on *Monday Night Raw*, *Friday Night SmackDown*, *WWE*
and *WWE Superstars*. All the competitors bring their "A" games for the pay-per-view events
most important of these annual events is WrestleMania.

ATTLES:
IEW EVENTS

le from all fifty states and countries around the world
d the live broadcast of WrestleMania! Millions more
h it on pay-per-view. Other big events like the Royal
ble and SummerSlam have long histories in WWE, too.
ging Rights, another pay-per-view event, features a battle
een *Raw* and *SmackDown*. Events like Elimination
mber and TLC are known for their tough matchups that
ly involve tables, ladders, chairs, and cages! In the WWE
erse, pay-per-view events are the real deal.

In the mid-1980s, Mr. McMahon was hard at work. He wanted to take WWE's brand of sports entertainment to the top of the industry. He had already collected the best mix of wrestling talent from the old territories and was finally ready to take the next step. That next step was the creation of WrestleMania, the biggest event ever in sports entertainment! It brought together stars from music, television, movies, and sports who performed their own acts during the show in between matches that featured the best WWE Superstars. WrestleMania and other big events like it were the future of the wrestling business.

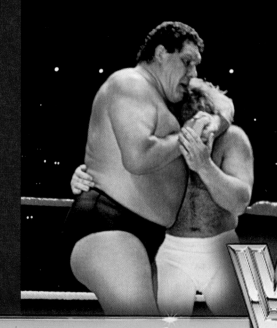

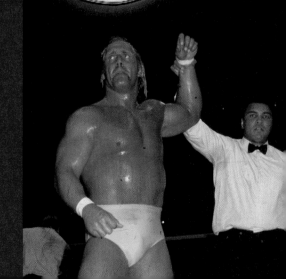

The first WrestleMania was held at New York City's famous Madison Square Garden and was headlined by "Rowdy" Roddy Piper and "Cowboy" Bob Orton. They fought against their greatest foes, including Hulk Hogan, "Superfly" Jimmy Snuka, and Hollywood star Mr. T. Legends like Muhammad Ali were ringside for the epic match. The first WrestleMania was broadcast to small movie theaters around the country over closed-circuit television because at the time, home pay-per-view was not available.

estleMania sent shock waves through all of sports entertainment. Never before had a sports tertainment event brought in such big names! No wrestling event had been on live national television fore, either. Mr. McMahon's gamble had paid off! From that point forward, WWE was changed ever. Since then, WrestleMania has become the biggest event WWE produces every year.

It's not surprising that since WrestleMania was so successful, Mr. McMahon wanted to ho
another one! But he decided that this WrestleMania event—WrestleMania 2—should be held in thr
locations—New York, Chicago, and Los Angeles. The New York City event featured a boxing mat
between WWE Hall of Famer "Rowdy" Roddy Piper and actor Mr. T! In Chicago, WWE Hall of Famer And
the Giant competed in a massive battle royal with WWE Superstars *and* gridiron greats from the NI
In Los Angeles, Hulk Hogan faced King Kong Bundy in a steel cage. WrestleMania 2 proved that the fi
event wasn't just a fluke—WrestleMania was here to stay.

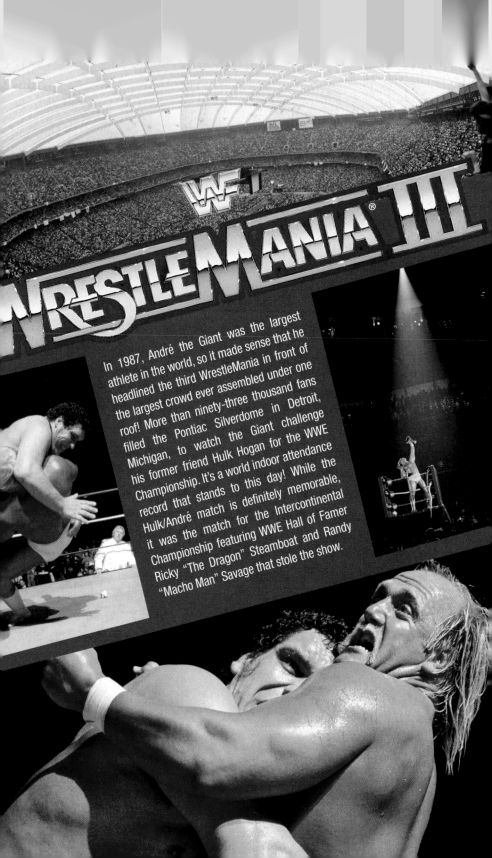

WRESTLEMANIA III

In 1987, André the Giant was the largest athlete in the world, so it made sense that he headlined the third WrestleMania in front of the largest crowd ever assembled under one roof! More than ninety-three thousand fans filled the Pontiac Silverdome in Detroit, Michigan, to watch the Giant challenge his former friend Hulk Hogan for the WWE Championship. It's a world indoor attendance record that stands to this day! While the Hulk/André match is definitely memorable, it was the match for the Intercontinental Championship featuring WWE Hall of Famer Ricky "The Dragon" Steamboat and Randy "Macho Man" Savage that stole the show.

WrestleMania IV was held in 1988 at Atlantic City's Trump Plaza. It featured a WWE Championship tournament. André the Giant had been stripped of the title for trying to sell it to "Million Dollar Man" Ted DiBiase. At WrestleMania IV, more than a dozen WWE Superstars came together to compete for the vacant championship. DiBiase and Randy "Macho Man" Savage outlasted the other competitors and battled each other in the tournament finals. Savage eventually defeated DiBiase to capture the gold while Donald Trump looked on from ringside. After his victory, Macho Man celebrated in the ring with his beautiful manager, Miss Elizabeth.

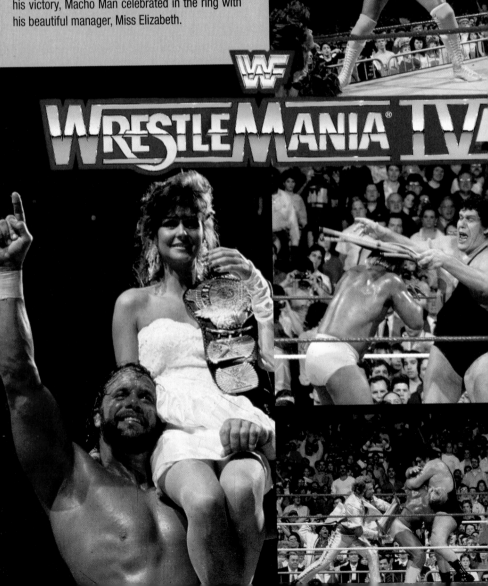

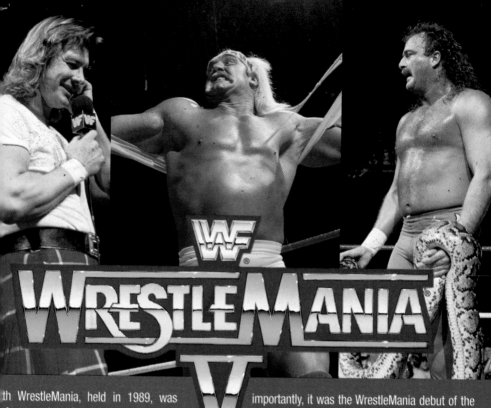

th WrestleMania, held in 1989, was
for a number of reasons, including
t that it was the first and only
Mania to be held in the same location, Trump
or the second year in a row. The main event
d the two former members of the Mega Powers
m—Hulk Hogan and Randy Savage—who
ach other for the WWE Championship. But most
importantly, it was the WrestleMania debut of the
man who would one day come to be
known as Mr. WrestleMania: Shawn
Michaels! Michaels and his tag team partner Marty
Jannetty competed against the Twin Towers, Akeem
and the Big Boss Man. In WrestleMania events to come,
Shawn Michaels would become the most popular
Superstar at the event.

The first time WrestleMania was held outside the United States was in 1990. The event took place in Toronto, Canada. The Intercontinental Champion Ultimate Warrior battled WWE Champion Hulk Hogan in a Title vs. Title Match that ended with the Warrior becoming WWE Champion! There were a lot of special guests in attendance, like Mary Tyler Moore, Robert Goulet, and Steve Allen. Plus, fan favorite André the Giant competed in his final match. And guess who watched the event as a spectator? Future WWE Superstar, Edge!

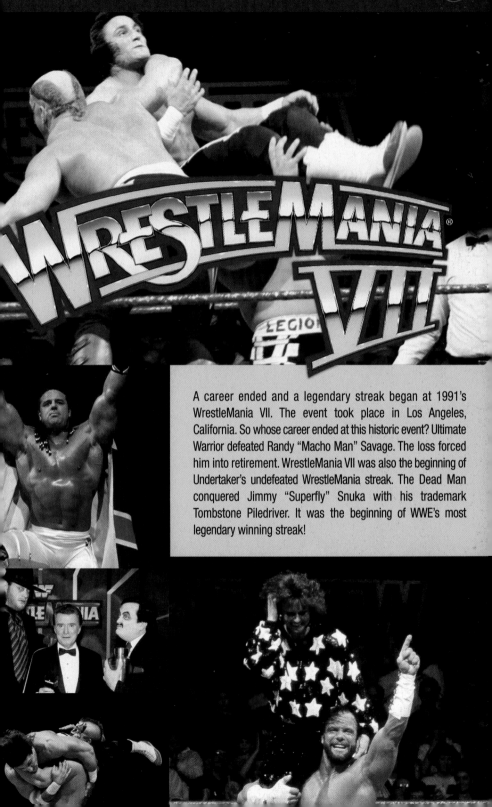

A career ended and a legendary streak began at 1991's WrestleMania VII. The event took place in Los Angeles, California. So whose career ended at this historic event? Ultimate Warrior defeated Randy "Macho Man" Savage. The loss forced him into retirement. WrestleMania VII was also the beginning of Undertaker's undefeated WrestleMania streak. The Dead Man conquered Jimmy "Superfly" Snuka with his trademark Tombstone Piledriver. It was the beginning of WWE's most legendary winning streak!

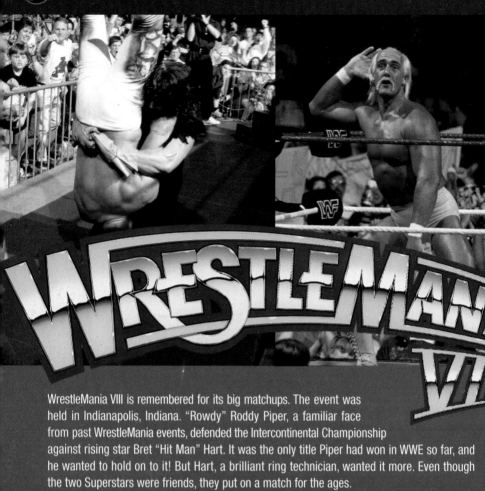

WrestleMania VIII is remembered for its big matchups. The event was held in Indianapolis, Indiana. "Rowdy" Roddy Piper, a familiar face from past WrestleMania events, defended the Intercontinental Championship against rising star Bret "Hit Man" Hart. It was the only title Piper had won in WWE so far, and he wanted to hold on to it! But Hart, a brilliant ring technician, wanted it more. Even though the two Superstars were friends, they put on a match for the ages.

Held at Caesar's Palace in Las Vegas, Nevada, this was the first WrestleMania staged outdoors. WWE Hall of Famer Jim Ross joined WWE that night, calling the action for the first time from ringside. WWE Champion Bret Hart lost his title to the giant Yokozuna, but Hart had his revenge when Yokozuna lost the title just a few minutes later to Hulk Hogan!

In 1994, a decade after the first WrestleMania, the biggest show of the year returned to the place where it all began—Madison Square Garden. It was here that Shawn Michaels cemented his place as "Mr. WrestleMania," competing in the first-ever Ladder Match at WrestleMania. This Ladder Match set the standard for all matches to come in the future. It was a revolutionary event, and it made Shawn Michaels a name everybody remembered.

Ladder Match: In a Ladder Match, an object (usually a championship belt, but sometimes something else, like a contract for a match or money) is hung above the ring. The winner of the match is the first to get the object. But the object is hung high enough that the Superstars need to use a ladder to get to it. The Superstars fight to be the first one to climb the ladder and grab the prize. What makes these matches so exciting? The ladder can be used as a weapon, too!

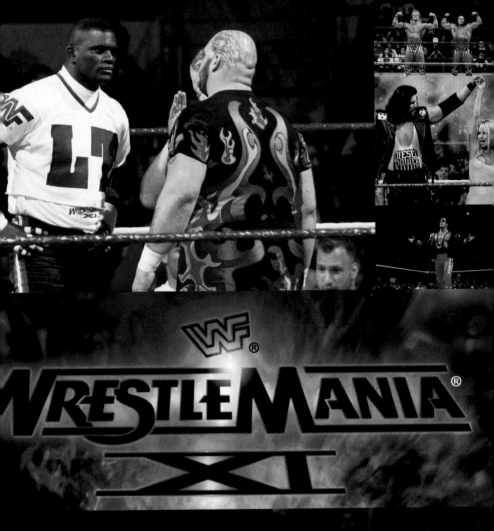

leMania always had amazing guest stars from the
ainment industry. These guests appeared onstage for
mances and never competed themselves. But in
an outsider competed in a main event match at
leMania for the first time! Football great Lawrence
, known as L.T., stepped into the ring to take on WWE
star Bam Bam Bigelow. Because he knew that
ow was aligned with the dangerous Million Dollar
ration run by Hall of Famer Ted DiBiase, L.T. didn't
alone. Several of his pro football friends joined him
de and protected L.T. from Bigelow and his dangerous
! It turned out to be a smart strategy because L.T.
he match!

The WWE Championship is the biggest prize in all of sports entertainment. WrestleMania is the biggest eve
WWE. And WrestleMania XII featured the biggest WWE Championship match *ever* at a WrestleMania! Supe
Shawn Michaels was known for his talent in the ring. Bret Hart was the "Excellence of Execution." The
competitors were fierce rivals. Put it all together, and you've got an unforgettable WWE Iron Man M
The rules were simple: Whoever had the most pins or submissions at the end of an hour would be \
Champion. But Michaels and Hart were so good, neither man had a victory when the hour was up. Michaels
in sudden-death overtime with a surprise pin on Bret Hart, earning him his first WWE Championship.

By 1997, WWE was loudly proclaiming its new attitude, and WrestleMania 13 in Chicago was the best place to show it off. A series of intense matches featuring a new generation of WWE Superstars like "Stone Cold" Steve Austin, Triple H, and The Rock took center stage at the biggest event of the year. Undertaker continued his winning streak and captured the WWE Championship. Bret "Hit Man" Hart made his last WrestleMania appearance—at least until WrestleMania XXVI. Hart won a Submission Match against Austin when Stone Cold refused to submit to Hart's sharpshooter, and eventually passed out because of the pain!

At WrestleMania XIV, "Stone Cold" Steve Austin had tons of fans supporting him in his quest to become WWE Champion. Fans loved Austin because he broke the rules and stood up to authority. The current WWE Champion, Shawn Michaels, had just joined forces with his best friend Triple H. Together, the two men formed D-Generation X. That's why the stakes were already high when Austin and Michaels faced off in the ring for the title of WWE Champion. Guest referee Mike Tyson just made the event even better! Austin pinned Michaels, and Tyson counted to three. Stone Cold was the new champion! It was the beginning of a new era in WWE: the Austin Era.

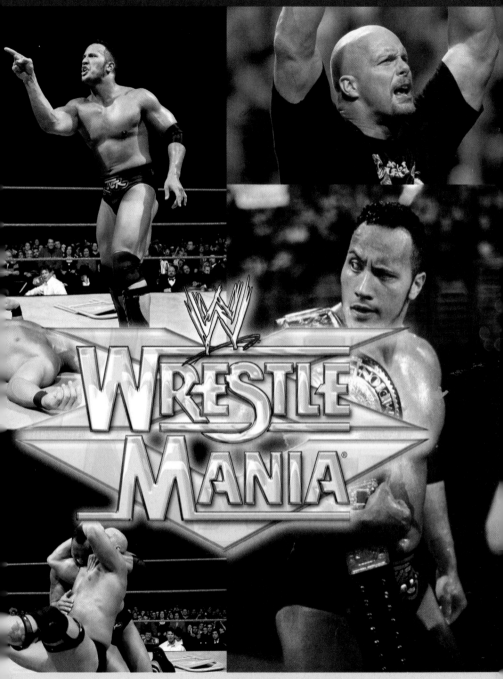

fore WrestleMania XV, Mr. McMahon formed his own team of talented Superstars called the
rporation. He wanted to fully control WWE, and he thought this was the way to do it. The biggest
perstar in the Corporation was The Rock, who was the current WWE Champion. "Stone Cold" Steve
stin hated the Corporation and fought against Mr. McMahon's goons whenever he could. At
estleMania XV, Austin beat up the entire Corporation, until only The Rock was left in the ring. In the
d, good prevailed over evil, and Austin defeated The Rock and took home the WWE Championship.

The year 2000 marked a new millennium—and an explosive WrestleMania! The McMahon family ha
grown apart since their days building WWE up in the 1980s. Now they hated one another! Ea
person in the family was desperate to control the family business so they could run things t
way they wanted. At WrestleMania 2000, each member of the McMahon family handpicked a WV
Superstar to represent them in the ring. Triple H, backed by his wife, Stephanie, and The Rock, w
had been picked by Mr. McMahon, squared off as the final two competitors in the four-man mat
Stephanie and Triple H—and the entire WWE Universe!—were shocked when Mr. McMahon turned
The Rock at the last minute, guaranteeing victory for Triple H.

se rivalries were the main focus of the ﾠteenth annual WrestleMania. One intense ﾠ, in particular: The Rock and "Stone Cold" ﾠAustin. Two years before, The Rock and ﾠCold tore the house down in the main ﾠat WrestleMania XV. But their rematch ﾠSeven was even more incredible! Austin ﾠnce again the winner of the match—and ﾠWWE Championship. He won because ﾠned forces with his most hated foe, Mr. ﾠhon. Mr. McMahon had a unique match ﾠown that night, too—a street fight with ﾠn! Mr. McMahon lost that match, though. ﾠeMania X-Seven will forever be ﾠbered as the night Vince McMahon ﾠn his own son and united with his worst ﾠ, "Stone Cold" Steve Austin.

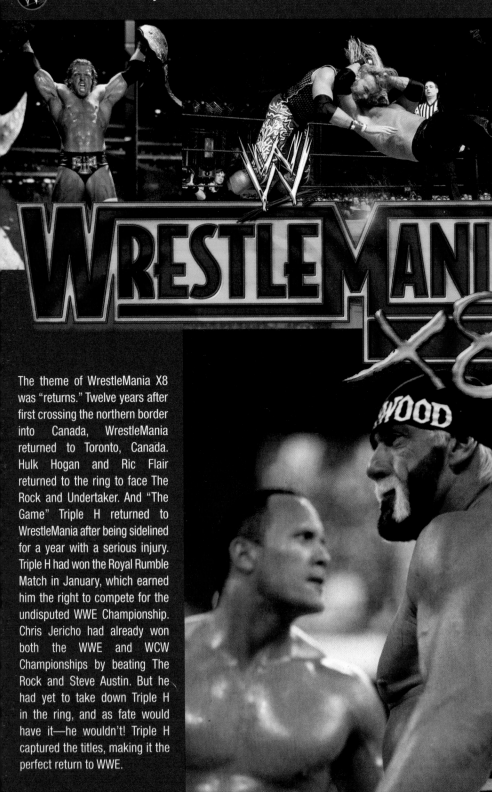

The theme of WrestleMania X8 was "returns." Twelve years after first crossing the northern border into Canada, WrestleMania returned to Toronto, Canada. Hulk Hogan and Ric Flair returned to the ring to face The Rock and Undertaker. And "The Game" Triple H returned to WrestleMania after being sidelined for a year with a serious injury. Triple H had won the Royal Rumble Match in January, which earned him the right to compete for the undisputed WWE Championship. Chris Jericho had already won both the WWE and WCW Championships by beating The Rock and Steve Austin. But he had yet to take down Triple H in the ring, and as fate would have it—he wouldn't! Triple H captured the titles, making it the perfect return to WWE.

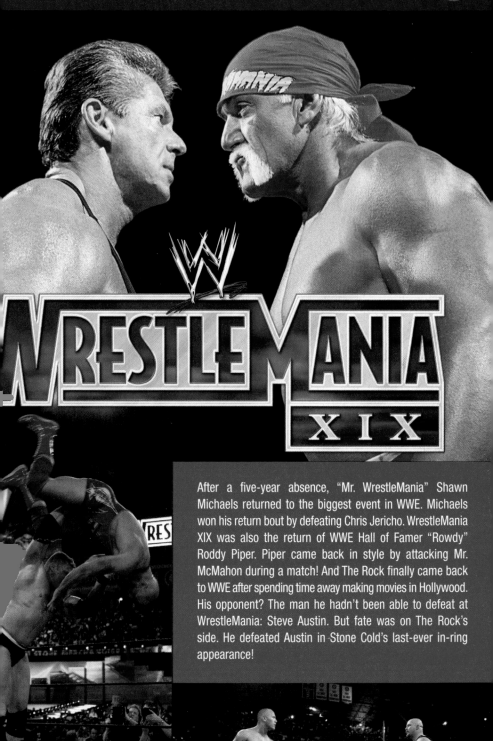

WRESTLEMANIA XIX

After a five-year absence, "Mr. WrestleMania" Shawn Michaels returned to the biggest event in WWE. Michaels won his return bout by defeating Chris Jericho. WrestleMania XIX was also the return of WWE Hall of Famer "Rowdy" Roddy Piper. Piper came back in style by attacking Mr. McMahon during a match! And The Rock finally came back to WWE after spending time away making movies in Hollywood. His opponent? The man he hadn't been able to defeat at WrestleMania: Steve Austin. But fate was on The Rock's side. He defeated Austin in Stone Cold's last-ever in-ring appearance!

It was hard to believe that two decades had
since WWE held the first WrestleMania, but it had
wanted to make WrestleMania XX an eve
remember. The slogan of the event was "Whe
begins, again." WrestleMania XX was held at M
Square Garden, the site of the first-ever Wrestle
Undertaker returned to WWE after his disappea
few months earlier when he'd been buried aliv
end of a match. Undertaker came back
vengeance and captured his twelfth Wrest
victory, this time over his half brother, Kane.
Cold" Steve Austin acted as a referee—b
attacked the match's two competitors! And
WWE Superstar named John Cena captured
title in WWE by winning the United States Champ

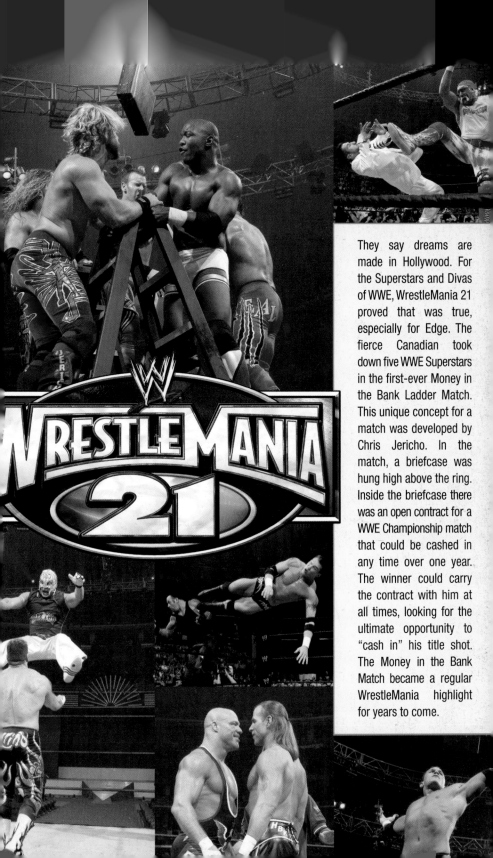

They say dreams are made in Hollywood. For the Superstars and Divas of WWE, WrestleMania 21 proved that was true, especially for Edge. The fierce Canadian took down five WWE Superstars in the first-ever Money in the Bank Ladder Match. This unique concept for a match was developed by Chris Jericho. In the match, a briefcase was hung high above the ring. Inside the briefcase there was an open contract for a WWE Championship match that could be cashed in any time over one year. The winner could carry the contract with him at all times, looking for the ultimate opportunity to "cash in" his title shot. The Money in the Bank Match became a regular WrestleMania highlight for years to come.

Even though WrestleMania 22 was the third WrestleMania to take place in Chicago, it was still a nigh firsts. Rey Mysterio became the smallest World Heavyweight Champion in history by defeating Ra Orton and Kurt Angle. Rey dedicated his victory to his best friend, the late Eddie Guerrero. McMahon faced Shawn Michaels in a brutal street fight. It was an intense match, but Micha eventually defeated the WWE chairman for the first time. And John Cena held on to his W Championship title by forcing Triple H to tap out thanks to his painful STF submission hold.

WRESTLEMANIA® 23 ™

Twenty years after setting a world indoor attendance record, WrestleMania went back to Detroit, Michigan. The arena in Motor City was the only place big enough to hold a pair of giant egos with even bigger bank accounts: Mr. McMahon and Donald Trump! Trump and Mr. McMahon had done business together in the past, but their business at WrestleMania 23 was a first for both of the moguls. Each billionaire selected a WWE Superstar to represent him in a match, and the losing billionaire would have to shave his head! Thanks to a little help from special referee "Stone Cold" Steve Austin, Trump's team won. So Trump and Austin forced McMahon into a barber chair and shaved off all of the WWE chairman's hair!

Florida has a special place in the history of sports entertainment. Some of the greatest Superstars and Hall of Famers got their start in the Sunshine State. So it was perfect that Florida was picked to host WrestleMania. Sixteen-Time World Champion Ric Flair retired in front of the WWE Universe. Big Show battled boxing Champion Floyd "Money" Mayweather. The Rock returned to WWE to induct both his father and grandfather into the Hall of Fame. And Undertaker extended his unbelievable winning streak to 16–0 by defeating Edge and winning the World Heavyweight Championship.

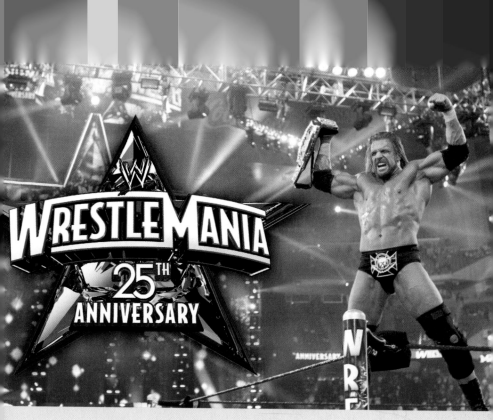

09, the WWE Universe came together to celebrate twenty-five years of WrestleMania. To kick off the ~ration, twenty-five WWE Divas competed in a battle royal. Hall of Famers Ricky "The Dragon" Steamboat, ~dy" Roddy Piper, and "Superfly" Jimmy Snuka joined forces to take on Chris Jericho. Undertaker and ~n Michaels put on an intense match that wowed the audience with lots of high-flying action and ~eholds. Crowd favorite CM Punk became the first Superstar to win the Money in the Bank Ladder Match ~ears in a row. Triple H defeated Randy Orton, keeping his WWE Championship. And John Cena once ~ became World Heavyweight Champion by beating both Edge and Big Show.

Battle Royal: A match where all the competitors are in the ring at once. A competitor is eliminated when they are thrown out of the ring. The last person in the ring is the winner.

WRESTLEMANIA XXVI

WrestleMania XXVI, in Phoenix, Arizona, was all returns and departures: the rise of new Superstars like Jack Swagger and the WrestleMania icon Shawn Michaels. It wa incredible night that thrilled fans throughout the Universe. Jack Swagger won the Money in the Ladder Match and convinced fans that he real the future of WWE. Bret Hart finally got his reve Mr. McMahon. More than a decade after the chairman had forced the Hit Man out of WW returned with a vengeance and defeated h enemy. And Jericho held off Edge, though l suffered from Edge's painful spear.

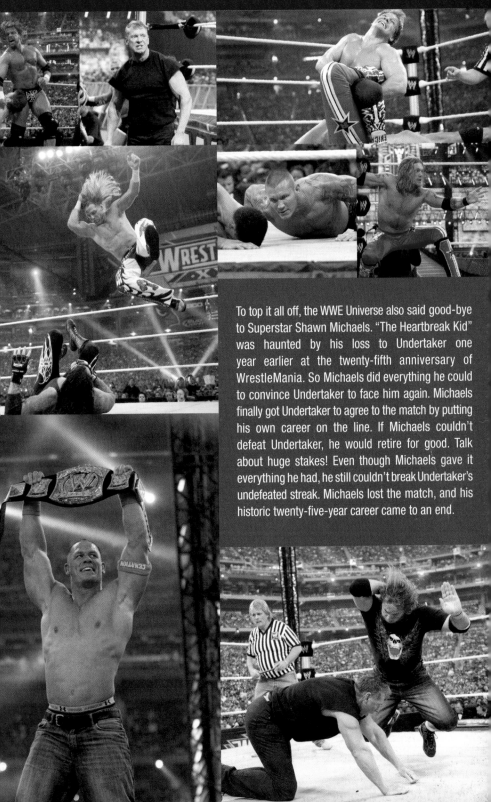

To top it all off, the WWE Universe also said good-bye to Superstar Shawn Michaels. "The Heartbreak Kid" was haunted by his loss to Undertaker one year earlier at the twenty-fifth anniversary of WrestleMania. So Michaels did everything he could to convince Undertaker to face him again. Michaels finally got Undertaker to agree to the match by putting his own career on the line. If Michaels couldn't defeat Undertaker, he would retire for good. Talk about huge stakes! Even though Michaels gave it everything he had, he still couldn't break Undertaker's undefeated streak. Michaels lost the match, and his historic twenty-five-year career came to an end.

W ROYAL

The Royal Rumble is one of the most exciting and unpredictable events in WWE. Every January, thirty WWE Superstars compete for the chance to go to WrestleMania and face the World Champion. In 2011, the number of entrants was upped to forty—the largest Royal Rumble match in history!

The rules are simple. Two WWE Superstars start in the ring, and every ninety seconds, a new man enters. A Superstar is eliminated when he is thrown over the top rope and lands on the mats below, with both feet touching the floor. The order that the Superstars enter the ring is random, but sometimes it's assigned by Mr. McMahon as a prize for winning a match on *Raw* or *SmackDown*.

The Royal Rumble has had a lot of memorable moments over the years. Fans remember that it was the first time WWE Hall of Famer "The American Dream" Dusty Rhodes competed in a tag team match with his son Dustin. Another fan favorite was the match where Sergeant Slaughter won the WWE Championship by defeating the Ultimate Warrior. And who can forget when Mr. McMahon won the 1999 Royal Rumble!

RUMBLE ®

are a few fun facts about the Royal Rumble.

Royal Rumble victories:
e Cold" Steve Austin (3 times)

est Royal Rumble time:
Mysterio (1:02:12)

est Royal Rumble time:
no Marella (0:00:01)

eliminations in a single Royal Rumble:
(11 Superstars)

iest entrance number: 27

Divas who have competed in the Royal Rumble:
na and Beth Phoenix)

SUMMER SLAM

The hottest event of the summer is WWE's SummerSlam. The first event was held in 1998 in New York's most famous arena, Madison Square Garden. It was there that the Ultimate Warrior put an end to the Honky Tonk Man's record run as the Intercontinental Champion. Since then, this pay-per-view extravaganza has been home to many memorable matches.

The Legion of Doom (Road Warrior Hawk and Road Warrior Animal) won its first WWE Tag Team Championship at the 1991 SummerSlam. This victory made it the only tag team in sports entertainment to win the titles in the AWA, NWA, and WWE!

In 1992, SummerSlam moved to London, England. Nearly ninety thousand WWE fans filled the arena to see the main event between Bret "Hit Man" Hart and "The British Bulldog" Davey Boy Smith.

No fan can forget the final SummerSlam event of the 1990s. It was there that WWE Hall of Fame inductee Jesse "The Body" Ventura, who was also the governor of Minnesota at the time, acted as a special referee in the main event.

SummerSlam amazed fans throughout the twenty-first century, too. Fans remember when Undertaker chokeslammed JBL through the roof of a limo and Triple H outlasted five other competitors in the dangerous Elimination Chamber. This was also when Randy Orton became the youngest World Heavyweight Champion in history. SummerSlam was the first time John Cena and Batista squared off, which led to Cena getting seriously injured—he had a broken neck that required surgery! And Triple H took on the Punjabi Nightmare, the Great Khali.

To this day, SummerSlam continues to be a phenomenal summertime tradition for fans across the WWE Universe.

Survivor Series was originally held on Thanksgiving night and featured tag team elimination bouts. But as time passed, the focus of the Survivor Series moved from tag teams to one-on-one matches.

In the mid-1990s, Survivor Series stopped being held on Thanksgiving night, but it still took place in late November. By then, WWE Superstars like Shawn Michaels, Bret Hart, and Undertaker competed in matches at Survivor Series, which made the event prestigious. Survivor Series was where Undertaker won his first WWE Championship.

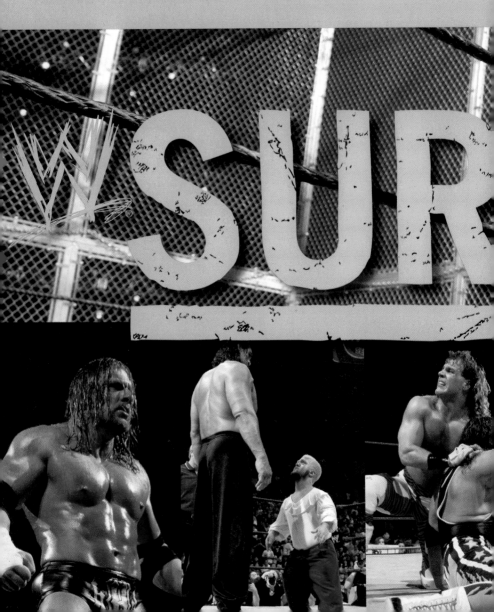

The most famous and talked about Survivor Series took place in 1997 in Montreal, Canada. The main event was WWE Champion Bret "Hit Man" Hart against Shawn Michaels. Hart was planning to leave WWE for WCW, and this was his last match, so he wanted to win. But Mr. McMahon had other plans. Worried that the Hit Man would steal the WWE Championship belt and make fun of it on WCW's TV show, the chairman ordered a referee to end the match early and awarded the title to Michaels!

n the mid-1990s, there was a lot more aggression and action in the ring throughout all of sports entertainment. WWE Superstars ignored the rules of the match and went after their opponents with all the tricks that they had, even if they weren't egal! This was how ECW and the WWE's Hardcore Championships were born. Since then, the rules have been more strictly enforced in other WWE matches. But one night a year, all bets are off, and the WWE Superstars have a chance to show heir hardcore skills at Extreme Rules.

RULES™

Extreme Rules is a one-night event where there are no rules, except for a few that are specific to each match, like No Holds Barred (where any weapon, move, or even other people are okay to use against your opponent) or Falls Count Anywhere (where a Superstar can lose the match by being pinned anywhere, not just in the ring). The WWE Superstars can use whatever weapons they can get their hands on. Superstars definitely bring, and feel, the pain! Extreme Rules is exciting, but it is also very dangerous. Do *not* try this at home!

HELL IN A CELL

When a rivalry *really* heats up between a pair of WWE Superstars, it can often lead to a Steel Cage Match. And when they have to settle a rivalry, Superstars face off in Hell in a Cell. The cell is a gigantic chain-link cage that covers the entire ring and the mats on the floor. The cell is two stories tall! Every year, WWE holds a series of matches in the cell.

TLC

TABLES | LADDERS | CHAIRS

...he rest of the world, TLC stands for "tender,
...g care." But not in WWE! In WWE, those
...rs mean "tables, ladders, and chairs." It's an
...ing, high-flying, hard-hitting annual event.
...y match features a table, ladder, or chair
...art of the Superstars' arsenal of moves.
...etimes all three are included in a single
...h! Originally TLC Matches were held at
...stleMania and SummerSlam and featured
...or four tag teams vying for the tag team
...But those matches were so fun to watch
...WWE gave them their own yearly
...per-view event.

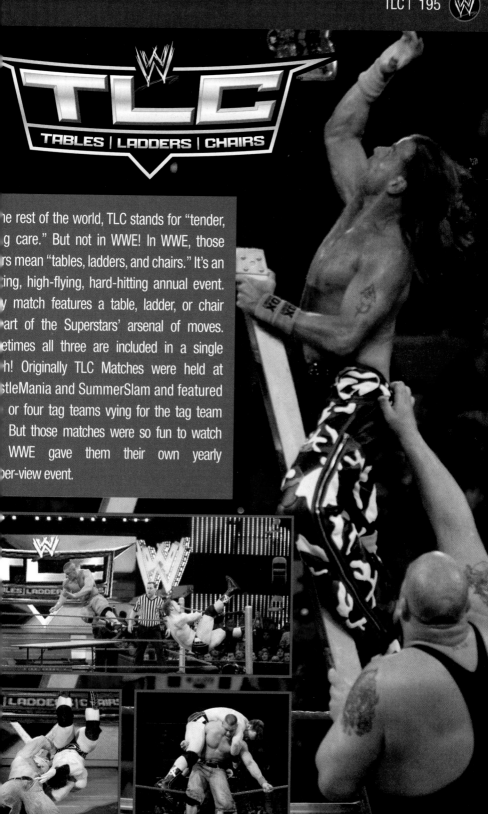

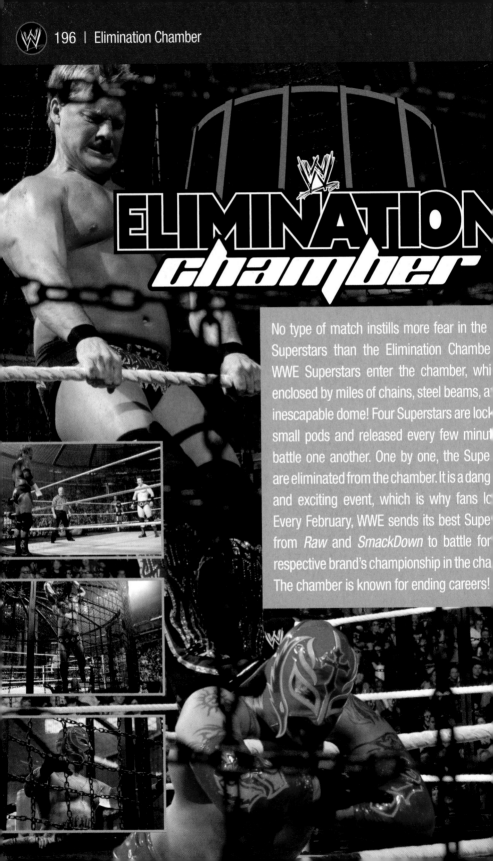

ELIMINATION chamber

No type of match instills more fear in the
Superstars than the Elimination Chambe[r]
WWE Superstars enter the chamber, whi[ch]
enclosed by miles of chains, steel beams, a[nd]
inescapable dome! Four Superstars are lock[ed]
small pods and released every few minut[es]
battle one another. One by one, the Supe[rstars]
are eliminated from the chamber. It is a dang[erous]
and exciting event, which is why fans lo[ve]
Every February, WWE sends its best Supe[rstars]
from *Raw* and *SmackDown* to battle for
respective brand's championship in the cha[mber]
The chamber is known for ending careers!

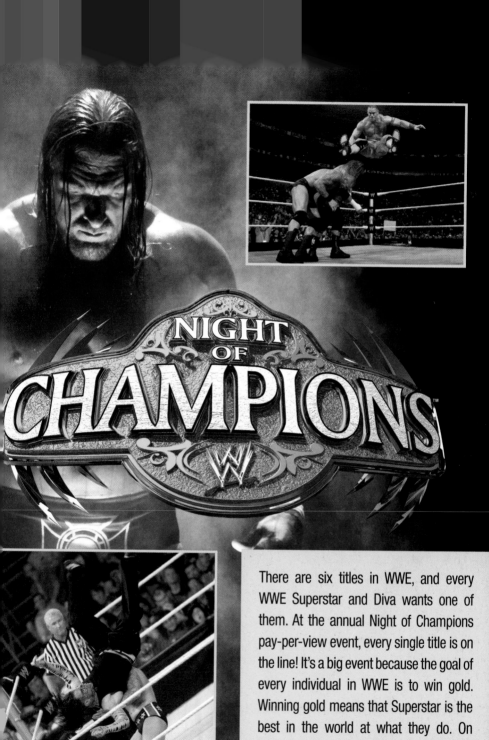

NIGHT OF CHAMPIONS

There are six titles in WWE, and every WWE Superstar and Diva wants one of them. At the annual Night of Champions pay-per-view event, every single title is on the line! It's a big event because the goal of every individual in WWE is to win gold. Winning gold means that Superstar is the best in the world at what they do. On the Night of Champions, Superstars and Divas are able to add their names to the prestigious—but short!—list of individuals to have held the championship titles. There is no greater honor in WWE.

MONEY IN THE BANK

Money in the Bank be
as a WrestleMania tradition, but
so popular that it eventually became its
pay-per-view event. In Money in the Bar
briefcase is suspended high above the rir
contains a contract allowing the winne
challenge for the WWE or World Heavywe
Championship at any time over the next y
The first Superstar to climb a ladder
retrieve the briefcase wins the match and
coveted prize inside. With the stakes as
as they are, the competitors will do anyt
to get the briefcase. And since ever
who's won Money in the Bank so far
successfully cashed it in for the champion
it's the most desired prize in WWE.

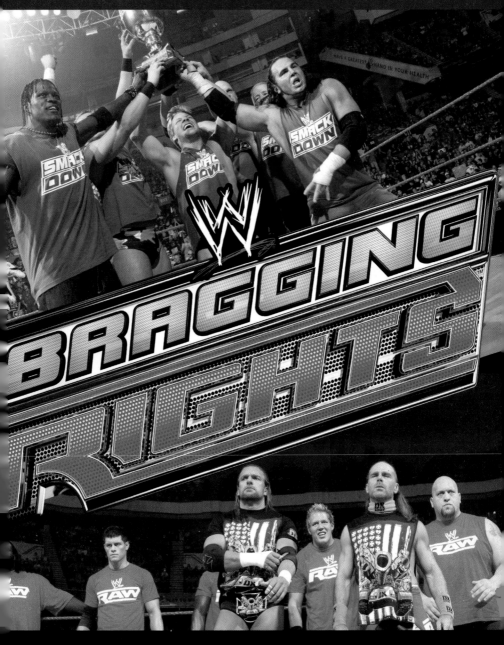

alry between *Raw* and *SmackDown* may not seem too intense at first. After all, the two brands
h part of the larger universe of WWE. However, the Superstars and Divas are extremely loyal
home brand and will defend its honor at all costs! Bragging Rights is the best place to do just
l the matches on Bragging Rights feature competitors from *Raw* squaring off against their
nts from *SmackDown*. It's not about championships or titles. It's about pride and showing the
niverse that your brand is the best in all of sports entertainment.

WrestleMania may be the night the WWE Universe looks forward to every year, but the *night before* isn't so bad, either! That's when WWE inducts its newest members into the Hall of Fame and honors the stars who have helped build WWE over the last fifty years. From those who established the territories to those who made sports entertainment what it is today, the Hall of Fame is loaded with all-time greats whose accomplishments are nearly impossible to top. Induction into the Hall of Fame is the greatest honor in WWE.

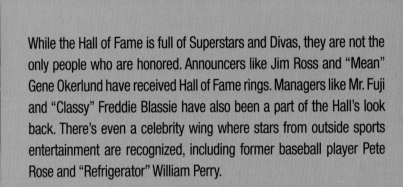

While the Hall of Fame is full of Superstars and Divas, they are not the only people who are honored. Announcers like Jim Ross and "Mean" Gene Okerlund have received Hall of Fame rings. Managers like Mr. Fuji and "Classy" Freddie Blassie have also been a part of the Hall's look back. There's even a celebrity wing where stars from outside sports entertainment are recognized, including former baseball player Pete Rose and "Refrigerator" William Perry.

SHAWN MICHAELS

HEIGHT: 6 feet 1 inch
WEIGHT: 225 pounds
FROM: San Antonio, Texas

SIGNATURE MOVE: Sweet Chin Music

ACCOMPLISHMENTS:
WWE Champion, World Heavyweight Champion, Royal Rumble Winner (1995 and 1996), Intercontinental Champion, World Tag Team Champion, Unified WWE Tag Team Champion, European Champion

Few WWE Superstars have accomplished as much in careers as Shawn Michaels. For more than twenty Michaels wowed his fans all over the world with his spect skills. Michaels started his career in the American Wr Alliance (AWA) in the late 1980s. The proud Texan was a m of the Rockers, a popular tag team that also included Janetty. Michaels eventually split from Janetty and be known as "The Heartbreak Kid."

After joining WWE in 1988, Michaels rose through the ra become one of the icons of the company. The WWE Un calls him Mr. WrestleMania because he has had more matches at that event than any other WWE Superstar! H defeated all-time greats like Bret Hart and Ric Flair. Duri time in WWE, Michaels earned his nickname of "Showsto Michaels said good-bye to sports entertainment after his match with Undertaker at WrestleMania XXVI. His in-ring may be over, but the WWE Universe has not seen the Shawn Michaels.

DX

TEAM MEMBERS: Triple H,
Shawn Michaels,
Hornswoggle (mascot)

FORMED: 1997

WWE's rebellious attitude changed sports entertainment. Colorful characters like the silly clown Doink and the lovable Tugboat were long gone. Angry and defiant Superstars emerged in their places— Superstars like D-Generation X, a team that consisted of Shawn Michaels and Triple H. DX gave fans many moments to remember, including ignoring the orders of former WWE commissioner Sergeant Slaughter and pretending to battle each other for the European Championship! An injury forced Shawn Michaels out of the ring for several years, and everyone thought that was the end of DX. But eventually Triple H and Michaels reunited.

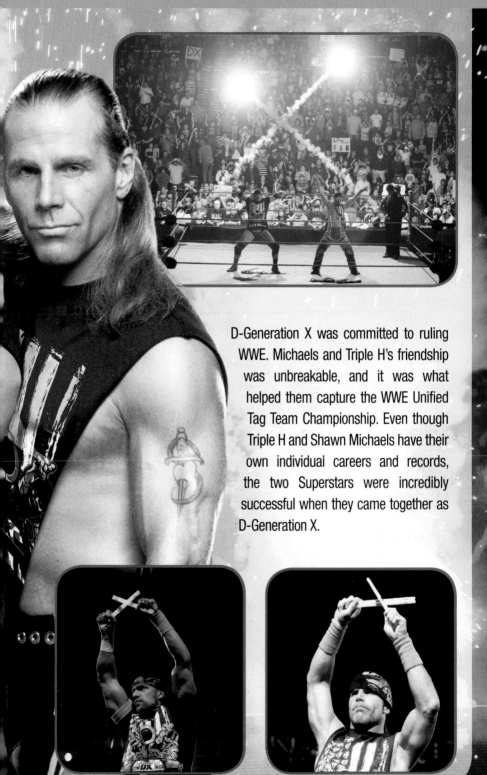

D-Generation X was committed to ruling WWE. Michaels and Triple H's friendship was unbreakable, and it was what helped them capture the WWE Unified Tag Team Championship. Even though Triple H and Shawn Michaels have their own individual careers and records, the two Superstars were incredibly successful when they came together as D-Generation X.

BATISTA

HEIGHT: 6 feet 6 inches
WEIGHT: 290 pounds
FROM: Washington, D.C.

SIGNATURE MOVE: Batista Bomb

ACCOMPLISHMENTS:
WWE Champion, World Heavyweight Champion, WWE Tag Team Champion, World Tag Team Champion, Royal Rumble Winner (2005)

Batista has the perfect nickname—the Animal! Thanks to his short temper and a tough mean streak, the Animal won championship after championship. Even though he was once associated with Triple H and Randy Orton in the team Evolution, Batista conquered WWE all on his own. He is a lone wolf, and a hungry and dangerous one at that!

Some of the greatest WWE Superstars in history have felt Batista's wrath. He took on—and defeated—some of the WWE's biggest stars, including Undertaker, John Cena, Triple H, and Hall of Famer Bret "Hit Man" Hart. Even Batista's "friends" weren't safe! Batista lived to be the World Champion, and nothing stood in his way of winning the gold. Once the Animal had been unleashed, there was no way to get him back in his cage!

André the Giant

André the Giant was known as the Eighth Wonder of the World. No wonder—he was the larges athlete to ever compete in a sports entertainment ring! André the Giant was also the very firs WWE Superstar to be inducted into the Hall of Fame. The famed Frenchman made his nam competing in events in every territory around the world. He traveled all over Europe and eve to Japan. A one-time WWE Champion, Andre's most famous moment came when h faced Hulk Hogan in the main event at WrestleMania III. The match took place in front of ove ninety-three thousand fans live in the Pontiac Silverdome.

André's Measurements: André the Giant was a massive individual. He stood 7 feet 4 inche and weighed well over five hundred pounds!

"Stone Cold" Steve Austin

...he 1990s, WWE was the most popular it had ever been, thanks to Superstar "Stone Cold" Steve ...tin. Austin started his career in WCW and ECW, where he earned a small but loyal fan following. ...when he joined WWE, he became one of the biggest stars in its history! Fans remember him for ...egendary rivalries with Bret Hart and Vince McMahon. Austin was known as a rebel who wasn't ...id to play by his own rules. Since retiring from the ring, he's even become a Hollywood celebrity.

"The American Dream
Dusty Rhodes

The son of a plumber, Dusty Rhodes grew up longing to live the American Dream of fame a
fortune. And Rhodes did eventually represent the American Dream. He rose up from nothing a
achieved greatness in sports entertainment. A multi-time World Heavyweight Champion in the N\
Rhodes had a ton of skills and charisma in the ring. Rhodes was also known for his contributi
behind the scenes. He helped put together some of the most popular and successful matches a
events in sports entertainment history! His legacy is carried on by his sons, current WWE st
Goldust and Cody Rhodes.

"Rowdy" Roddy Piper

"Rowdy" Roddy Piper has fought for everything he's ever had. After he left home at only thirteen years old, the fiery Scot began training for and competing in-ring. Piper had a forty-year career with many highlights. He was one of a select few to have been in the main event at both WrestleMania and the NWA/WCW mega event, Starrcade. He boxed Mr. T, wrestled Bret Hart, and fought Greg Valentine in a brutal Dog Collar Match. His trademark kilt and bagpipe music always told the WWE Universe that something exciting and unpredictable was on its way.

Bret "Hit Man" Hart

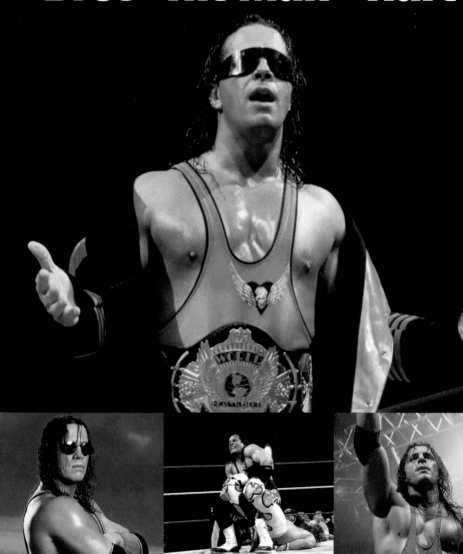

Bret "Hit Man" Hart called himself "the best there is, the best there was, and the best there ever be." It was a bold claim, but Hart backed it up every time he entered the ring. Hart was a brill technical wrestler and was one of only three WWE Hall of Famers to have held both the WWE WCW Championships. Thanks to the training he received from his father and fellow Hall of Fam Stu Hart, Hart headlined WWE events for almost ten years and usually defeated his opponents. matches with Steve Austin and Shawn Michaels were unforgettable, and so were his family fe with Davey Boy Smith and Owen Hart.

Ricky "The Dragon" Steamboat

WrestleMania III, over ninety-three thousand members of the WWE Universe watched in awe as cky "The Dragon" Steamboat and Randy "Macho Man" Savage stole the show in a match for the ercontinental Championship. It was a high point in Steamboat's career. Only a couple of years er that show-stealing performance, "The Dragon" captured the NWA World Heavyweight ampionship in a series of legendary matches with Ric Flair. Steamboat now helps train a rising neration of Superstars.

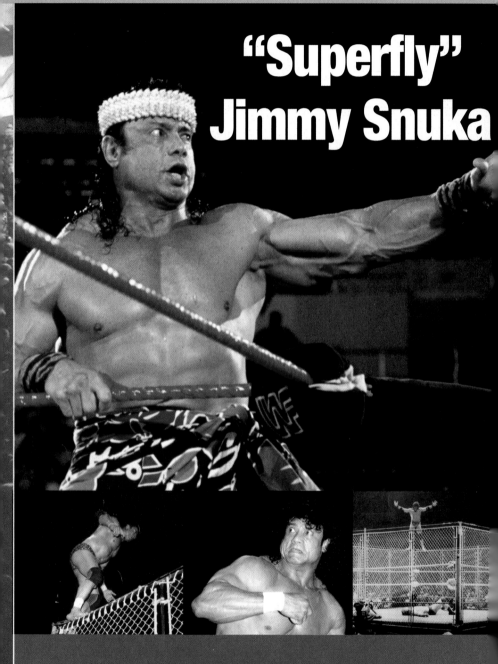

"Superfly" Jimmy Snuka

Long before cruiserweights like Rey Mysterio and Evan Bourne took to the skies with their high-flying wrestling moves, there was "Superfly" Jimmy Snuka. The barefooted Superstar from Fiji was a true pioneer. He was famous for his dives from the top of steel cages and splashes from the top ring rope. Snuka was part of a great Polynesian family and is related to greats like the Wild Samoans and The Rock. He was even a part of the first WrestleMania, where he was the first victim in the Undertaker's legendary WrestleMania streak!

"Cowboy" Bob Orton

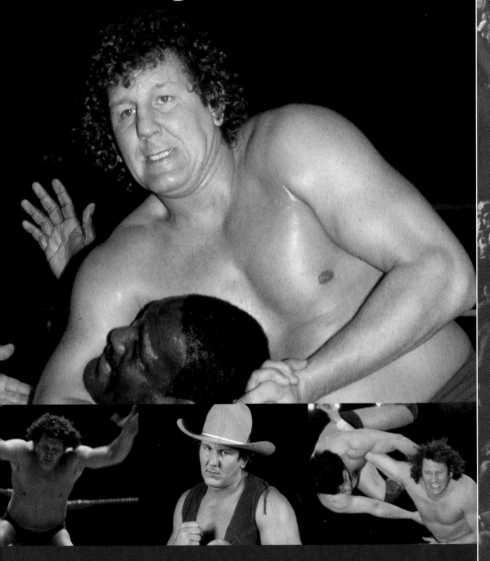

"Cowboy" Bob Orton is remembered for his broken arm that never healed! He wore a cast in the ring for years and used it as a weapon against his opponents. A second-generation Superstar, Cowboy (also known as Ace) traveled the road with "Rowdy" Roddy Piper. He served as Piper's bodyguard and tag team partner. The duo was in the main event at the first WrestleMania and was rarely seen apart. Ace is proud of his accomplishments in WWE, but he is even more proud of his son, Superstar Randy Orton.

Eddie Guerrero

Sports entertainment was in Eddie Guerrero's blood. The late WWE Champion's family ran a wrestli[ng] territory in El Paso, Texas, and Mexico. Growing up in that environment gave Eddie the skills he needed [to] succeed in ECW, WCW, and WWE. Whether it was pure technical wrestling or high-flying cruiserweight acti[on,] Eddie amazed the WWE Universe with his talent. Eddie will never be forgotten by the WWE Universe.

Sergeant Slaughter

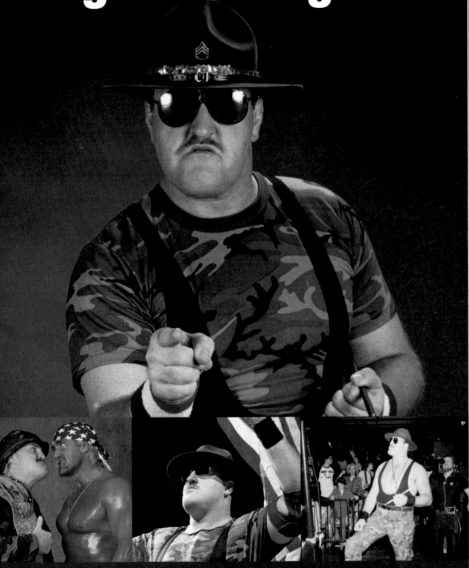

rgeant Slaughter accepted his Hall of Fame induction wearing a camouflage tuxedo and his trademark drill rgeant hat. Slaughter closed an amazing WWE career by calling the Hall of Fame audience to attention. The mer WWE Champion was known for being fiercely patriotic. Sergeant Slaughter was an American marine ho accepted a position in the WWE offices after retiring from the ring. Slaughter acted as the WWE mmissioner, who was responsible for setting up exciting matches. Slaughter commands respect from the VE Universe wherever he goes. *And that's an order!*

"Million Dollar Man" Ted DiBiase

"Everybody has a price for the Million Dollar Man." That phrase, along with his arrogant laugh, earned DiBiase the hatred of the WWE Universe through the 1980s and 1990s. Ted DiBiase was a spoiled rich man with a selfish attitude, and he brought that attitude with him to WWE. He once tried to buy the WWE Championship from André the Giant! When that failed, he created the diamond-studded Million Dollar Championship belt to show off his riches. But the former World Tag Team Champion could outwrestle his opponents and was successful at training future WWE Superstars, including his son, who also goes by the name of Ted DiBiase. "The Million Dollar Man" may have taken a lot from sports entertainment, but he's given back a lot, too.

Tony Atlas

Atlas was a powerhouse superstar in the 1970s and 1980s. With the help of his tag team partner y Johnson (father of former WWE Superstar The Rock), Atlas was the first African American World eam Champion in history. Despite being retired from the ring, Atlas makes sure to stay in shape.

Pat Patterson

Pat Patterson is best known as being the first WWE Intercontinental Champion, a title that he won in 19
Brazil. But that is only one accomplishment from Patterson's long, successful career. Outside of his ama
in-ring career, Pat has also acted as a color commentator on WWE programming. He has helped y
Superstars develop their talent and worked alongside Mr. McMahon as a WWE executive. Few people
WWE and sports entertainment as much as Pat Patterson. He has truly made WWE his life's work.

Jim Ross

world of sports entertainment would be a very different place if not for Good Ol' JR, Jim Ross. The best
orts entertainment announcer to ever get behind a microphone, JR has called some of the greatest moments
WWE history. A sports entertainment veteran of more than thirty years, JR has worked as the lead announcer
he WCW and on *Raw* and *SmackDown* in WWE. JR's passion and skills behind the mic have earned him the
e and respect of the WWE Universe.